AmuseD
by innovation
Let your muse inspire you!

By Keith Bourgoin

The quick and dirty guide to create new exciting ideas and energize innovation in your business.

AmuseD by Innovation

AmuseD by Innovation, Second Edition.

Copyright © 2026 by Keith Bourgoin

All rights reserved. No part of this book shall be reproduced, stored in a retrieval system, or transmitted by any means, electronic, mechanical, photocopying, recording, or otherwise, without written permission from the publisher. Any product mentioned in this book does not represent an endorsement and is purely used for example purposes. No patent liability is assumed with respect to the use of the information contained herein. Although every precaution has been taken in the preparation of this book, the publisher and author assume no responsibility for errors or omissions. Neither is any liability assumed for damages resulting from the use of information contained herein.

Note: This publication contains the opinions and ideas of its author. It is intended to provide helpful and informative material on the subject matter covered. It is sold with the understanding that the author and publisher are not engaged in rendering professional services in the book. If the reader requires assistance or advice, a mandated professional should be consulted.

The author and publisher specifically disclaim any responsibility for any liability, loss or risk, personal or otherwise, which is incurred as a consequence, directly or indirectly, of the use and application of any of the contents in this book.

Table of Contents

Introduction 9
    Step into the unknown..9
    The future is flexible..11
    Are you open-minded?..12
    Name that tune in one 13
    To err is human, to dare is divine..14
    Innovation or "transnovation" 15
    Responsible innovation 16
    The Fourth Industrial Revolution 16
    Who I am 18
    How this book is structured 19
    Acknowledgments..19
Part 1 – Why some fish swim upstream..21
    Summary 21
    Chapter 1 – Wine ages well, businesses not so much 22
        Topics covered 22
        A bit of history..22
        The boy who cried "wolf"..23
        Kids discarding matches to play with Plutonium 24
        Chapter Summary 25
    Chapter 2 – The journey is the destination.......................................26
        Topics covered 26

- A bit of history 26
- Carpe diem 28
- Talent is a community strength 28
- More than the sum of its parts 30
- Chapter Summary 30

Chapter 3 – Impossible is a self-fulfilling prophecy 32
- Topics covered 32
- A bit of history 32
- Is impossible even a word? 33
- Let's meet at the next crossroad 33
- Chapter Summary 34

Part 2 - The shortcut to far, far away 35
- Summary 35

Chapter 4 – The science of introspection: know thyself 36
- Topics covered 36
- A bit of history 36
- The missing link and the archaeologist 37
- Ask the oracle 38
- Chapter Summary 39

Chapter 5 – Breaking the mold is only the beginning 40
- Topics covered 40
- A bit of history 40
- Survival of the fittest 41
- Let's play Follow the leader 42
- Challenge yourself before someone else does 43

Get some fashion-sense	44
Chapter Summary	44
Chapter 6 – Learn to play and play to learn	**46**
Topics covered	46
A bit of history	46
The deep side of the pool with floaters	47
Build it and they will come	48
Keep up the good work	49
Chapter Summary	50
Part 3 – Cockroaches and entropy	**52**
Summary	52
Chapter 7 – Carving stairs in the mountain	**53**
Topics covered	53
A bit of history	53
Make me one with everything	54
Ultimate simulation: let's hit 88 mph!	55
Chapter Summary	55
Chapter 8 – Meditate the meaning of Life	**56**
Topics covered	56
A bit of history	56
The right angle to every circle	57
Namaste to you too	58
Mature to realize your mantra	59
Chapter Summary	60
Chapter 9 – Location, location, location	**61**

Topics covered	61
A bit of history	61
Let's play "Where's Waldo?"	62
Reinventing transportation, Sci-Fi style	63
Chapter Summary	64
Chapter 10 – Are we there yet?	65
Topics covered	65
A bit of history	65
The times, they are a-changin'	66
Hurry up, we're waiting	67
Reading in the tea leaves	68
Chapter Summary	69
Chapter 11 – Going off-road	70
Topics covered	70
A bit of history (sort of)	70
How to use the cards	72
Two innovation methodologies	73
Resource optimization and efficiency	74
Processes & operations optimization and efficiency	86
Chapter Summary	104
Chapter 12 – Who, tell me who	105
Topics covered	105
A bit of history	105
Hello, is it me you're looking for?	106
Deus ex Machina	107

If you act now, I will double your offer 108

Swipe right if you like me 110

Chapter Summary 110

Chapter 13 – An obstacle course covered with landmines 112

Topics covered 112

A bit of history 112

Playing catch with nail guns 114

A budget leak is not the same as cash flow 115

I sense a disturbance in the force 116

Crash test dummies in a car full of airbags 117

License to thrill 118

Obstacles can slow you down but never stop you 119

Chapter Summary 119

Part 4 – Something new, something blue… 121

Summary 121

Chapter 14 – Interdimensional travels 122

Topics covered 122

A bit of history 122

Multidimensional thinking 122

Innovation is continuous improvement on steroids 124

Wash, rinse, repeat 125

The Fair shooting gallery 126

True innovation is a chimera 127

Anticipation instead of provocation 128

Third time's the charm 128

AmuseD by Innovation

- Chapter Summary 129
- Chapter 15 – Making this a social affair 130
  - Topics covered 130
  - A bit of history 130
  - Partnerships and Frenemies 131
  - Fear of failure is success underachieved 133
  - Procrastination is the cancer of success 134
  - Innovation is something exciting, never seen before 135
  - Chapter Summary 136
- Chapter 16 – Pin the tail on the donkey 137
  - Topics covered 137
  - A bit of history 137
  - Light a fire with a spark (not literally) 137
  - Ten times a googolplex 138
  - Imagination is about having time to dream 139
  - Sciences and the Arts 140
  - The OMG method 142
  - Playing with the baseball cards in chapter 11 143
  - Innovation inspiration workshop ideas 144
  - Chapter Summary 147
- References 148
  - Glossary 151

Introduction

Step into the unknown

Imagine for a moment that you are navigating the open sea. Suddenly, you spot a sliver on the horizon. You look at your map and your GPS but cannot identify it. With precaution, you decide to investigate. As you get closer, you realize that it is indeed an island, an uncharted piece of land recently surfaced and somehow still unknown. "Land! Land!" You want to yell with excitement. You carefully bring your ship to shore and secure it in place. You step off on the sandy beach, and, with pride, you claim your discovery: "I name this land PoppedOutOfNowhere Land!" (It's my land, I can name it as I fancy).

It's a big deal. You were the first, you get to claim ownership and settle on it before anyone else can. That gives you unprecedented advantage.

When you venture into new territory, everybody else plays catch up.

Innovation, the subject of this book, is quite similar; when you innovate, you are entering a virgin territory where you get to raise your castle first. You call the shots; you're the master of your domain. When everybody starts following you, you have already moved to the next stage by planning improvements. Business is the same as colonizing; if it gets overcrowded and it becomes harder to set up residence where you are, you move to new land where nobody is around.

I am a firm believer that if you own a business and want to succeed, you need to spend every day thinking about improvements. Innovation is just another tool to improve. How is this different than continuous improvement? The way I distinguish the two is by looking at improving something that already exists or introducing something new. Continuous improvement is expected and simply relies on the resources and methods you have in place that will be refined with the experience you gain. Introducing a new resource with unique attributes or changing a fundamental process by replacing it or adding layers to it, that's innovation. It requires investigating the right

---

AS KNOWLEDGE INCREASES, WONDER DEEPENS. - CHARLES MORGAN

component that will best fit this new requirement. Innovation is a change with unpredictable results that is aimed at delivering a new benefit.

Except that innovation is hard, very hard. You need to stay ahead of the game, sustain your creativity. In the meantime, competitors keep appearing with fresh new ideas to challenge you, taking advantage of state-of-the-art technology always more accessible. Customers get bored much faster and demand new experiences every day. How can you keep up and constantly reinvent yourself?

Well, you are in the right place to answer these questions. This book will provide you with the assets to develop competitive products and services that are unique and provocative. It was developed for a single purpose: to trigger new ideas that may be out of your comfort zone because innovation is all about trying new things.

So how do we start? Innovation starts with inspiration, the "secret weapon" of any innovation initiative. Thomas A. Edison was quoted in the September 1932 edition of Harper's Monthly Magazine saying that *"genius is one percent inspiration and ninety-nine percent perspiration"*, (www.phrases.org.uk, s.d.). He evidently never lived through a writer's block, staring desperately at the dreadful blank page, because he would know that inspiration requires a tremendous amount of energy.

Knowing how to tap into inspiration is the real challenge.

Inspiration is defined as *"something that makes someone want to do something or that gives someone an idea about what to do or create: a force or influence that inspires someone"* (www.merriam-webster.com, s.d.). For some, inspiration comes naturally; they are artists and their muse always seems to be by their side. However, this book is designed to help everyone generate innovation and thus find inspiration. To assume that only artists can create is simply wrong and I will show you how to generate innovation ideas whether you have creation skills or not.

YOU CAN'T WAIT FOR INSPIRATION. YOU HAVE TO GO AFTER IT WITH A CLUB. - JACK LONDON

The future is flexible

The problem with developing innovation is that an organization grows with the inverse of its entropy – That's the law. Truly, as an organization become larger, it becomes more complex and requires more rules, structure, constraints. Innovation, on the other hand, requires a high degree of freedom or if you prefer entropy. Thus, logic proves that if organizations grow opposite to their entropy and entropy can be substituted for freedom to create, then logically an organization that grows will create less. Bummer.

Oddly, this is actually very reasonable. The constant introduction of more complex and structured processes to manage increasing levels of details reduces freedom by applying limits to change, thus avoiding dangerous instability. Don't get me wrong, following due process in official business is a necessity, much like the need to follow the scientific method when doing proper research. The problem is that energy expenditure grows exponentially with structured processes. This means that until you find a gold nugget, you can search for a gold mine a long time if you have to turn every rock. Rigor and discipline imposed by regulations have stiffened creativity to guarantee systematic accurate results.

Yet many great inventions and discoveries were often accidental. If every step was needed all the time, innovation's speed would be dramatically reduced. There needs to be a path to innovation freedom that will allow proper rigorous regulations following initial discovery.

As the tech bubble burst looms, reinvention will be key to restart this engine. We are bound to witness many failures, but we are also guaranteed to see, as it has always happened in the past, flamboyant misfits that will think outside the box and create the phoenix of new industries, born from the ashes of the old. If history has taught us anything, it is that the future is flexible.

AmuseD by Innovation

Are you open-minded?

I have said it; you will be traveling outside of your comfort zone. This means that you need to be open-minded to assume abstract concepts and agree that unless something is disproved, it remains possible. This is key to unlocking the creativity of free thinking. For this purpose, I propose an acid test for this book. I believe I may lose many readers on this next mind trip, but I beg you to make the effort to read further: this is not so much about agreeing with me as it is about the fact that you cannot disprove me completely. If you embrace possibilities, as small as they can be, then they are worth investigating. Onward with our little experiment.

Do you believe in Big Foot? Yes, I know. I did ask for an open mind. This requires some explanation. As you may know, Bigfoot is this legendary hominid also called Sasquatch or the Yeti who is presumed to be a primate very close to humans that has survived isolated in remote parts of the world. Like most people, you have most probably answered a definite "no" to this question. This answer is in line with what you know and feels right.

This is where we push the boundaries of our awareness, outside our comfort zone. What do we truly know about this subject, and do we have enough information to answer equivocally against this belief? Have we exhausted every bit of information to consider this an impossibility?

Personally, I am not ready to say that it exists, but I am not fully convinced that it doesn't either, considering the following discoveries/facts. You might be interested to know that until the 1930s, something as commonly accepted today as the giant panda was only a legend without substantial evidence (www.absolutepanda.com, s.d.). Go look it up, I'll wait...When it comes to giant primates, it is fascinating to know that the mountain gorilla was but a myth until a body was discovered in 1902, only about a century ago (www.wikipedia.org, s.d.). The truth is that we discover new species every year, even very large animals that should have been found by now yet remained completely undetected by modern technologies.

I'VE FAILED OVER AND OVER AND OVER AGAIN IN MY LIFE AND THAT IS WHY I SUCCEED. - MICHAEL JORDAN

AmuseD by Innovation

Can we truly discard the hypothesis that a huge population of giant hominids still remains undetected today? Statistically, we believe that there is a minimum size of population individuals to keep species alive so our reasoning is that they should be easy to spot if they existed. The main issue that we contend with is the fact that recent discoveries have given strength to the hypothesis that every homo species that has ever lived has shared its contemporary history with at least one other homo species (www.wikipedia.org, s.d.). In addition, we need to take into account the vast amount of forest land in the world that has never seen modern man (mentalfloss.com, s.d.). Considering the amount of world folklore around these mythical beasts spread from the Americas all the way to deep Asia (en.wikipedia.org, s.d.), can we absolutely confirm that we have enough evidence to prove that another homo species does not exist?

And now we are back from our experiment. This demonstrates that unless you managed to explore one hundred percent of a hypothesis, you cannot guarantee that its impossibility is a fact. This also implies that you should not accept generally accepted opinions at face-value until you have enough evidence to support a specific point of view.

Innovation is an unfamiliar territory, full of nay-sayers and people ready to kill your ideas before they are given the chance to be explored. It is your responsibility to sell your vision. This book will give you the tools to help you with this difficult task. Fight the urge to accept the obvious and keep an open mind to even the frivolous.

Name that tune in one

We have now established that I have very uncommon ideas (let's leave it at that). Because I sometimes go into a mental jamboree, thoughts tend to rearrange in my mind in very unusual ways. All this happens without the use of any illicit substance.

As I mentioned earlier, human reflex when landing on new ground is to claim it. I do the same by naming things I discover to help make sense of them and you may encounter some of my naming creations in this book. Without being

LORD, GRANT THAT I MAY ALWAYS DESIRE MORE THAN I CAN ACCOMPLISH. - MICHELANGELO

as adept with word transformation as Doctor Seuss was, I will often invent some new words to organize my thoughts, being a fan of etymology. You will find words invented for mnemonics or classification purposes. If this hurts your love of the English language, then I apologize for this "globerroneousblunder".

To err is human, to dare is divine

Speaking of word play, you have probably noticed that the naming of this book consists of two superimposed words: amused and muse. The etymology of the word amuse says it all: from the subtractive "a" and muse for passion, concentration. The definition of the word is *"to divert from serious business"* and this book should probably curb this to actually say "to divert from habitual/structured business". I cannot emphasize more the departure from standard business since I highly encourage to "play", to discover and experiment. You need to let loose to appreciate the great outdoors.

For inspiration and thus innovation to be triggered, it needs a generous amount of freedom and key ingredients: the proper medium, the right environment, an openhearted state of mind and suitable tools.

- **Medium:** a communication and collaboration scheme by which ideas flow and engagement is facilitated -- failure is acceptable.
- **Environment:** a place to promote innovation by triggering imagination -- through play, experimentation and asking questions.
- **State of mind:** be opened to new ideas, even if they seem strange at first; breaking established barriers is desirable.
- **Tools:** provide plenty of construction blocks and modeling vehicles (whiteboard, paper/pen, 3D visualization/printer, etc.)

And did I mention an unlimited amount of curiosity and courage? This is a game of "Truth or Dare" where everyone is incited to dare.

SUCCESS IS HOW HIGH YOU BOUNCE WHEN YOU HIT BOTTOM. - GEORGE S. PATTON

Innovation or "transnovation"

In my mind, I picture innovation (broken down as in-novation, for "inner" and "novation" for new) as the act to introduce something new within an existing concept. Because there is familiarity of the concept sprung from the evolution of the already established, the adoption is slightly easier.

When you create a brand-new product or experience that has no comparable before, its adoption cycle is much longer. Potential customers must first understand the value proposition of this newcomer, and it has a greater risk of market failure. This is often because this new offering addresses a need that the consumer may not yet have noticed; you must then sell the product and also explain how it fulfills this need. I have dubbed this unique process transnovation (broken down as trans-novation, for "trans" to transform the present and novation), a word I invented to distinguish this much more disruptive event, a revolution.

You must decide if you want evolution or revolution. It is essential that you decide this early because revolution is riskier and requires both massive R&D and marketing dollars. It this is a success though; you stand alone and develop a niche where you are years ahead of your competition. This is the story of many disruptors such as Apple's app store for iDevices and their micro-transactions, Google AdWords or Netflix. All these examples took years to convince the industry of their seriousness but in the end, created new markets in which they remained leaders for a long time because of their ground-breaking attitude and tenacity.

This book can inspire both innovation and transnovation. What you need to understand is that they need to be driven differently: innovation must answer the question "What does our product/service need today to meet the evolving needs of our customers (evolution)?" while transnovation must answer the question "What is the ignored/unknown need that potential customers may have or develop in the near future and how can we anticipate and fulfill it?"

THE CURE FOR BOREDOM IS CURIOSITY. THERE IS NO CURE FOR CURIOSITY. - ELLEN PARR

AmuseD by Innovation

Responsible innovation

Because innovation is one of the most change-inducing event people can experience, along with less tasteful scenarios like war or global disasters, it is essential that organizations consider the social repercussions of their innovations.

In her book *"Move: Putting America's Infrastructure Back in the Lead"* (Kanter, 2015), Rosaleth Moss Kanter explains the strategic challenge of developing public infrastructures (think roads for a city) for businesses, when infrastructure can be used by many services, some of which still undefined. This involves big unsolved problems with no clear market yet, so it is difficult to predict its profitability. As a matter of fact, profitability is often the immediate concern of the investment organization, but the ramifications of innovation can go well beyond the organization's sphere of influence. History is full of examples where innovation changed the way humans function and interact: the invention of cars, radios, televisions, computers and so on. These major breakthroughs spread like wildfire because of their huge benefits. Others also had detrimental effects such as some pesticides, the use of toxic insulation material or unregulated manipulation of radioactive materials.

More than ever, we need to be more responsible about innovation because communications, transportation and manufacturing are so efficient today that any innovation impact can grow exponentially fast, good or bad.

The Fourth Industrial Revolution

We are living what is called the third age of computing, the first age having been the mainframe era followed by client-server technology and now transformed by the advent of the cloud. While there is debate on what can be called an industrial revolution, the following markers are probably the most recognizable because of their significant impact on society (en.wikipedia.org, s.d.).

LOOKING AT THE HORIZON, I CANNOT SEE BEYOND BUT I KNOW IT'S THERE. I JUST GO FORWARD. - ME

1. **First Industrial Revolution:** the taming of nature-based power for industrial purposes (using water, wind and animals -- or in some unfortunate cases human slaves -- as raw accessible power to execute at scale); this launched the trade economy.
2. **Second Industrial Revolution:** the introduction of fueled machines capabilities; powerful, tireless and cheap; this announced the beginning of industrialization as we know it.
3. **Third Industrial Revolution:** I believe is the age of globalization with the advent of cheap worldwide transportation, effectively spreading work across the globe for obvious economic advantages and creating new world-based assembly processes.

The current Industrial Revolution is the commodity of artificial intelligence, provided at a quality level that rivals or bests humans; this essentially rewrites the rules of automation as both physical and software robots are effectively less expensive than globalization. This also signals the end of human-restricted knowledge/skill-based jobs to morph into more useful, richer roles for humans as robot teachers and overseeing responsibilities. In this age, human intelligence is there to direct or assist autonomous machines, not just as a cheap computation ability. There is increasingly little need to expose humans to danger since robots or drones can take these risks 24/7 for huge ROI gains. Humans' unique capabilities such as dynamic adjustments (mind agility) and creativity are becoming the most required job skills in the world.

This is an evolution of industrialization where we do not need to build the same items in large quantities to achieve efficiency, you only need to build what is required as you need it. As machines become more helpful, they also become more autonomous; worldwide communications are becoming machine-based with humans' interactions representing a subset of this channel (albeit an essential one). The rules of economics are again being rewritten since jobs and roles are fundamentally affected -- on a global scale. Even countries that have been heavily dependent on affordable human labor during the globalization of the industrial revolution are now turning to automation to readjust their business model.

Who I am

You may wonder why I am so passionate about innovation. My background may explain why I have always been an outsider, thinking out of the box.

I own a university degree in microbiology but never actually practiced. While attending university, I worked part-time in computer technology, which I believed at the time would be essential to manage the "big data" that was coming from DNA sequencing. Unfortunately, I was about ten years too early since the most significant use of computers in this field at the time was predominantly word processing. Seeing as computers were offering me a more promising future than the laboratory, I went on to start my thirty years' career in information technology (IT).

I started at Apple Computers in the technical response group (the "genius bar" of the time) and went on to gradually engage with ever more complex computer service environments. Over the years, I worked on datacenters management and conception, introducing groundbreaking technologies such as virtualization and active systems monitoring. I am now a cloud and mobility planning architect. I have a reputation of being a technology modernisation junky with a pragmatic approach to problem solving.

Now, I am above all an innovation advocate since product lifecycles, information dissemination time and offerings development schedules are all shrinking. As I have always been involved in improving processes in a fierce market of service consulting, I acquired a unique experience to improve and differentiate faster. Today, I work for Avanade, an Accenture joint venture with Microsoft, to support our clients in developing their innovation agenda through workshops and brainstorming sessions.

I have not invented the two-sided zipper nor am I a billionaire from Silicon Valley. I am however pretty good at making hard things easily accessible. I teach people how to dream, that's where I get my groove. I have been helping many people stuck in limbo to get pumped again and on the road to success. As a Canadian who knows how hard it is to get out of a snowbank, I can appreciate a complete stranger showing empathy to lend me their traction-aid to get out of trouble. So, I want you to think of this book as the Swiss army knife to pull you out of business boredom and get the proverbial push you need to get back in the lead.

How this book is structured

This book is structured into 4 parts.

Part 1 explains the rationale of innovation in today's market and explains why innovation results come as much from the journey as it does from the destination.

Part 2 is about pace of learning and awareness of change; external events that happen to your organization are just as fundamental as those that are lived internally and require special attention.

Part 3 is where we really dig deep into the questions that will nurture your inspiration dialogs and eventually support your innovation projects definitions.

Part 4 is all about the next steps, now that you own an innovation idea, to plan for unforeseen circumstances and implement the right approach to meet your goals.

Each chapter is introduced with a short story that is either a personal experience or something that I felt was relevant to share in order to help put things into context, hopefully establishing a mood to simplify the assimilation of abstract concepts. I often rely on satire because I believe it improves the clarity of the message (absurdity is great to distinguish the good from the bad) and it makes for more interesting reading.

Acknowledgments

This book would not have been possible without the support of some extraordinary people. I wish to thank my wonderful wife and my two

AmuseD by Innovation

extraordinary boys for all their help, patience and wild adventures. I wish to also thank my entourage and colleagues for giving me the wonderful opportunities I have had over the years in helping and teaching our clients to innovate; not everyone is fortunate enough to work in a field that just happens to be their passion. I want to acknowledge my close friends (you know who you are) who were always there to push me to exceed what I believed my limits were, only to show me how wrong I was. Finally, I would be forgetting an important part of my life if I did not mention the companies that have fueled my passion for innovation in my career such as Apple Computer, Microsoft and Accenture/Avanade; they believe in breaking new grounds and gave me the courage and craving to challenge the status quo.

I would also like to add that many references in this book are taken from one of the most valuable community projects today: Wikipedia. Please donate to support their continuous contribution in improving knowledge quality and accessibility.

And now, God speed.

AmuseD by Innovation

Part 1 – Why some fish swim upstream

"I tell you, Grak, we have no couple time anymore.
It went to his head after he invented the wheel..."

Summary

Innovation is not so much a strategy as it is a way of life. The hyper-competition of today and the high expectations of customers, constantly amazed by technology advancements, are making innovation a necessity for the survival of a business. The modern challenger must now always be on the lookout for disruptive predators ready to attack. This is healthy paranoia since customer indifference is equal to irrelevance. In this first part, we look at the motivation and the available techniques to stay ahead of the game.

AmuseD by Innovation

Chapter 1 – Wine ages well, businesses not so much

Topics covered

In this chapter, we will focus on understanding what the purpose of innovation is in the modern enterprise. With the technology strides that we are witnessing today, we will emphasize the urgency of developing an innovation agenda as more and more organizations are empowered to challenge and scale at tremendous speed, creating a competitive landscape never seen before.

A bit of history

My boys are Generation Z. They were born in the digital age and cannot conceive this modern world we live in without some kind of mobile device attached to the Internet and their interests. They call their friends by clicking on their images and often have multiple conversations at the same time. Their idea of relaxing is to connect to a cloud service and either play as a team on an online game or pull-in a video from the 'net.

I was born during the space race. My first experience with getting a document copy was from an alcohol-based photocopier, which made a two-toned bluish washed-out image of the original. Back then, we changed channels on a TV by turning a dial (attached to the television, no remote in sight) to one of a handful of channels. It was also the way we called friends and neighbours, only one at a time, by dialing their number on a rotary telephone (thankfully, we only had to deal with seven digits) which was itself bound to a wall by a cord. We then scheduled some time to meet in the street to play dodge ball and other stuff.

In between these forty years or so, something happened that changed the world. First, like many others, I was introduced to my first personal computer and home dot matrix printer. Suddenly, I was able to publish my own documents, with colour, from the comfort of my home. Then, I discovered bulletin board systems (BBS) and the Internet which opened new horizons for knowledge and exchange. But the coming of the web was the real revolution; the empowerment it gave to people was unprecedented.

IF OPPORTUNITY DOESN'T KNOCK, BUILD A DOOR. - MILTON BERLE

AmuseD by Innovation

When I started on one of my earliest IT jobs, I remember having a conversation about the potential of the web, at a time when the Internet catalogs like Yahoo and Alta Vista were on everybody's lips. A colleague of mine asked me if I shared his opinion that the web was a remarkable technology for information access. Without hesitation, I disagreed; I firmly believed that the web's strength was in publishing information, not accessing it. I guess I was not the only one who felt that way considering the Twitter, Instagram, Facebook, YouTube and other social networks that appeared after, creating a new powerful way of sharing opinions and experiences.

The digitally converged world of today is all about user empowerment. It enables people to find, access and connect with other individuals and things that was the realm of science-fiction not so long ago. Anyone now has the capability to change the world; this is the challenge and the opportunity. If sometimes you "feel" changes coming but ignore your instincts -- because you like the status quo, peaceful and secure – then it's probably because you need to do something about it.

The boy who cried "wolf"

I have been called an alarmist because I warn companies to wake up and step into the future before somebody else does. I suppose this can sound like an empty threat and thus, a while back, I decided to investigate if there was data to substantiate my warnings. It so happens that there is plenty of that around to support this therefore I thought I would share a few that are especially insightful to accurately picture the new extreme sport of company survival.

First, let's start with a bold statement: few organizations will survive the ten-year mark today. They may disappear because of attrition, customer churning, market evolution or even from a simple buy-out. One way or the other, their survival chances are comparable to the sandy beach hatched baby turtle and its slim chances of reaching maturity. Let's explore some numbers that demonstrate this volatility. According to Fortune Magazine,

---

WE AIM ABOVE THE MARK TO HIT THE MARK. - RALPH WALDO EMERSON

eighteen new companies appeared on the Fortune 500 index in 2015, a lot of them being digital challengers such as Netflix, Salesforce and Expedia. At the same time, we saw many organizations fall behind because of the slow adoption of a digital agenda (Fortune 500 2015, s.d.). Many of these challengers were not even in their competitors' rear-view mirror until it was too late.

The most fascinating information about all of this is that there is an actual mathematical model that can describe at which point a company cannot stay competitive anymore. Companies, like living things, can grow to a certain size before their organic structure requires a fundamental re-engineering, otherwise they face implosion. This is mainly explained by the fact that they evolve in a sublinear growth model, where the bigger they get, the more complex and inefficient they become. World-renowned physicist professor Geoffrey West and his colleagues studied this model, which is strangely analogous to the way life forms cannot grow bigger than a specific limit defined by the complexity increase of capillaries (Business Mortality, s.d.).

The study seems to demonstrate the need of organizations to reinvent themselves (re-engineer) or face the consequences. He co-wrote a paper called *"The Mortality of Companies"* in the *"Journal of the Royal Society Interface"* which basically defines how successful companies can eventually doom themselves due to the very same thing that made them successful: the success brought upon by modern ideas ultimately kills them because this success drives them to continue doing the same successful thing. This is the ouroboros conundrum of enterprise achievement.

Kids discarding matches to play with Plutonium
You are probably thinking that you know your business and your competitors better than me and I cannot possibly teach you anything about your market. I undeniably agree. What I am hinting at are the competitors that you don't know, the ones too small to see until they bite. You don't want to bring a knife to a gun fight with these aggressive little critters because they carry nuclear weapons.

ACTION IS THE FOUNDATIONAL KEY TO ALL SUCCESS. - PABLO PICASSO

AmuseD by Innovation

Today's modern technologies provide so much power for individuals who can harness it that it's a cage match with anyone willing to take you. The cloud, open-source technologies, Internet-based collaboration and on-demand manufacturing are dirt cheap and are rewriting the rules of fair engagement. Today's competition can crawl up from under a rock and scale exponentially to be a force to reckon with before you have time to realize the threat it poses to your business model.

In other words, we are seeing a technological revolution that is analogous to what Guttenberg did for the written word. As you may recall, before the printing press, Bibles were the possession of the rich since it took years for monks to painstakingly copy them by hand. This invention managed to capture this defenseless market with a technology that reduced effort by at least two factors of scale, effectively running the monks copying work out of business. What we are seeing happen today is a democratization of empowering technologies that open possibilities for self-publishing, global collaboration, customization and crowd funding on-demand and at scale. If you are the David of the Bible, your rock is weapons-grade plutonium. If you are Goliath, however, be afraid, be very afraid.

Chapter Summary
Modern technology empowers and unleashes capabilities that could only be dreamed of until recently. This provides opportunities to reenergize your company to enable it to create new success behaviors that purposely diverge from the traditional assets you are known for. This also means that the same power is available to much smaller and nimble organizations that aim to eat your lunch, capable to tap the same benefits and grow from unnoticeable to real threats very quickly.

YOU JUST CAN'T BEAT THE PERSON WHO NEVER GIVES UP. - BABE RUTH

AmuseD by Innovation

Chapter 2 – The journey is the destination

Topics covered

In this chapter, we will endeavor to demonstrate that innovation is not just about the end result but also about what you learn while you practice innovation. We will try to clarify why failure is acceptable as long as you progress in your development. Knowledge is power and knowledge shared is power at exponential levels. The discovery process of innovating, even from failure, can be positive if you gain something from the experience; the result may not always be the endpoint but in fact mostly the journey.

A bit of history

I mentioned earlier that innovating is a way of life. I probably should extrapolate on this by explaining that I believe innovating is mostly about introducing new things and that you never stop discovering and learning. And as long as you learn, you can apply that knowledge for many things; if it is not useful right away, that investment will mature later.

Let me tell you a story about a family vacation I had a while back.

My folks love new experiences; some of the best trips we had were totally spontaneous. There was this one time, I remember thinking that our family summer vacation needed to be glorious. However, I also wanted it to be special and different from our previous escapes. The kids had done Disney, almost an obligatory pilgrimage in America, where we flew from Montreal to Orlando, Florida. However, this pleasant three hours' flight was nowhere near equivalent to the experience I lived as a child, driving over thirty hours to the same destination during the Christmas Holidays. My unique child perspective, witnessing nature morph itself from snowbanks into tropical palm trees, was magical even before we sat foot in the fabled theme park.

This missed opportunity saddened me for my children and, knowing that with our modern busy lifestyle winter would have been an impractical time to travel, I opted for the alternative. I set out to find a place that would offer a very different landscape, even in summer, at a distance I could manage in

---

FAILURE IS THE KEY TO SUCCESS; EACH MISTAKE TEACHES US SOMETHING. - MORIHEI UESHIBA

a few days of driving. With a paper map, I used a ruler to measure twenty hours of highway trip and drew an arc to find the most interesting spots I hoped to discover. From Montreal, the one that won me over was Atlanta, Georgia. We had never been there, and I knew enough about the south of the United States to expect a change of scenery. A bit of reading about the location later, gathering information about the Coca-Cola and CNN museums as well as the famous Georgia Aquarium, were enough to convince us to hurl our ship towards undiscovered country.

The trip took two and a half days and a few stops along the way. I should probably mention that I am the turtle of this race, not the hare; I drive within the speed limit, which drives my Italian wife bonkers. The expedition was fascinating, crossing ten different states, so much so that the destination became almost prosaic. Even so, Atlanta and its many attractions were rewarding, with unique experiences that my children will never forget. Never before had we seen a rainfall that could almost carry us with it nor did we expect to defend our life against the distressing yet harmless cicadas! It was definitely memorable. The trip and its sudden flora transformation with its distinctive panorama and invasive kudzu, was the real vacation from the mundane. We even made a point of not taking the same road going in and out, just to see more.

The moral of this story is that we did not know what to expect from the destination, it was unknown and foreign to us. Despite this, we had a blast discovering all sorts of things completely alien to us; I even almost had the opportunity to eat alligator meat (I chose against it since I did not know if I could stomach it and I was the designated driver). Our destination could have been a disappointment, but it remains one of the most worthwhile vacation my family has ever had because the entire experience, including the voyage itself, was a special time that was meaningful and rewarding. Sometimes, the journey can be as stimulating as the destination, maybe even more.

IF YOU FELL DOWN YESTERDAY, STAND UP TODAY. - H. G. WELLS

AmuseD by Innovation

Carpe diem

To innovate is no different than a journey into the unknown, you have a vague idea of what to expect but cannot guarantee the result since you have never seen it yourself. Where it differs is that it is preferable to ensure some form of return on investment. Let's be clear: you will fail more often at innovating than you will achieve success. What this means is that you need to find gains in your failures; knowledge is by far the most valuable.

In Plato's Apology of Socrates, we understand how important it is to know the extent of what you do not know (Plato, s.d.). The process of exploring new experiences helps to define and clarify what we do know, possibly even gain more insight from it. The methods by which we refine our "ignorance" are by themselves rewarding, helping us to simplify, improve or accelerate research to heights never before realized; it is an occasion to rethink old concepts and methods.

This knowledge must remain in your organization and not belong to a single individual, to ensure that the committed investment serves the purpose of cultivating the consciousness of the business. In this scenario, failure is indeed acceptable as long as you learn from this advancement.

Talent is a community strength

I made a point in the last topic about the fact that knowledge needs to belong to a community, not a single individual. I have seen many innovation labs fail in their goals because projects were developed by individuals, something that usually does not benefit the organization. It is important to understand the difference between learning and assimilating.

The learning process of exploration should be celebrated and can definitely be assigned to single individuals as long as expectations of skill development are stated and understood. The innovation project and its research by-products however should be assimilated within the community and organization into the memory of the business, that it can be later retrieved

---

FAILURE WILL NEVER OVERTAKE ME IF MY DETERMINATION TO SUCCEED IS STRONG ENOUGH. - OG MANDINO

and possibly revisited. The reasoning of sharing a project journey is the same as sharing its ultimate goals and its success recognition.

I have noticed that the millennial generation is lightyears ahead of us in this field. They understand how to work in unison towards a specific goal, will share the spoils of war if they win and support each other when they face failure. This cohesive approach to building a social matrix of collaboration can be seen in how they behave in gaming, in real-life or in computers, by acting out campaigns that are highly successful in a pure democratic model.

I called this the Giza pyramid principle. In this framework, no single person wants to be responsible for the erection of this monumental engineering exploit. Yet everyone wants to be part of something meaningful and important because they can share the pride of this accomplishment. They are a cohesive community who believes in the strength of numbers to win together or supports itself in failure only to regroup and do better next time. This academic model of working as a single unit with no official leadership is known to be problematic with other generations but Gen Z has mastered it better than all its predecessors in my opinion.

Can we bottle this into a structure that can be reused and applied more generally? Possibly but the challenge is to transform the mindset of people to accept that gain is not in the individual's best interest but in the team's best interest, something that requires decades of deprogramming from the classic single individual evaluation model with the promotion that it entails. This has repercussions all the way to the CxO model of management which is bound to live a transformation in the next decade or so.

If the enterprise starts to quantify the ROI of fun and freedom of speech, I think it will become more generally accepted, provided that it comes with basic rules or respect and merit. At this point, we can expect to gain new levels of innovation effectiveness from having many generations of people working together: the experienced and skilled with the fresh effective untainted minds working as a collective with a shared knowledge and goal.

FAILURE IS SUCCESS IF WE LEARN FROM IT. - MALCOLM FORBES

More than the sum of its parts

In today's mindset of success-driven management, we thrive in accomplishments that have positive results with minimal investments. NASA has made strides in gaining tremendous amounts of scientific data from its explorations of Mars, the Jovian planets and even the dwarf planets Ceres and Pluto using only probes and robots. This data collection and transmission was highly effective in producing the results that were expected from these missions at a fraction of the costs of what would have been needed for manned missions, if they would have been possible at all.

In this view, the Apollo mission looks like a behemoth of investments for a limited amount of scientific data (moon rocks and some observations that robots and probes would be able to do today in a much more effective manner). But the program fostered an immense number of inventions that affected society for decades to come. Fifty years later, we are still using knowledge acquired during this process into design elements for the International Space Station and the coming Orion program. As a matter of fact, this research has had a profound effect at the social level on a global scale, even resulting in today's use of disposable absorbing diapers.

Clearly, knowledge gathered through innovation can be just as valuable as the innovation itself. Better yet, innovation shared can fork into other discoveries that are harder to measure in terms of return on investments because their impact can happen long after their introduction. One innovation project can bloom into many other child innovations that develop into a self-sustaining ecosystem, providing a unique opportunity to build an economic partnership with mutual investments and gains. Sometimes, an innovation's impact needs to be assessed with the ecosystem it pulls with it.

Chapter Summary

In this chapter, we attempted to demonstrate that failure is acceptable, which has often been dubbed the "fail fast" approach. However, failure without learning is a missed opportunity carrying the potential for large investments with little results because innovation discovery will necessarily result in more failures that successes. There needs to be an organization "memory" structured as a team of people, a repository of information or preferably both, that can ensure that knowledge remains within the business.

We also explored how the team structure can affect the way people perceive success and failure, especially with differences in generations of coworkers; it is a hot topic that requires rethinking fundamental human relations in the enterprise but holds very interesting potential.

Finally, we reviewed how innovation can have its own social structure. We explained how past failures can be turned into later successes and how synergy of improvements can become a force of its own. As you transform your business innovation from a single product or service into an ecosystem of partnerships, many more can benefit from it and also feed their own innovations in it, creating a self-sustaining economic model.

AmuseD by Innovation

Chapter 3 – Impossible is a self-fulfilling prophecy

Topics covered

In the previous chapters, we talked about the importance of innovating and how failure is not such a bad thing while developing your idea as long as you learn from your failure. In this chapter, we will focus on how you must keep your vision pure and your courage in adversity. I will present a less attractive aspect of innovation and try to prepare you for it. There may be moments when you question if this is worth it, which is why we started chapter one with this undisputable fact: innovation is a necessity. Your best ally in this is also your worst enemy: nobody can predict the future. The best we can hope for is to avoid disaster and play strategically.

Game on.

A bit of history

As a sci-fi geek, my mind is filled with stories taken from books, comics, TV and movies. One memory that is very fond to me is the first *Men in Black* movie, starring Will Smith and Sammy Lee Jones. I especially enjoyed the scene when the protagonist played by Will Smith is secretly recruited and goes through a psychology test, as part of the selection process for this elite group where only one will be chosen to be an agent.

The secret organization gives all candidates a paper test and a pen to answer a few skills questions, but he is the only one to ace the test. I will not tell you how if you haven't seen the movie but suffice it to say that he did it by thinking different: he does not accept the parameters that are given to him to work with and, without a second thought, decides to change the rules of the game and give himself an "unfair" advantage. It's only unfair if it is clearly forbidden. The lack of vision of your competition is their loss and your advantage.

This is what it's all about. Do not overthink about what you can or are allowed to do but why you need to do it, to reach your goal. The goal is all that matters, no matter how you get there. All roads lead to Rome.

THE LIMITS OF THE POSSIBLE CAN ONLY BE DEFINED BY GOING BEYOND THEM INTO THE IMPOSSIBLE. - ARTHUR C. CLARKE

AmuseD by Innovation

Is impossible even a word?

Here is another law for you. What is defined as impossible eventually is proven wrong – impossible is thus itself impossible given enough time and resources to disprove it. I guess you could call this a recursive theorem since the impossible is an impossibility according to this law. Mind blown.

Given that you must accept that anything said to be impossible will eventually be made possible, the only variables you need to consider are time and resources. Think for a moment at the work that has been dedicated to make man fly. It took centuries, if you start counting as early as Leonardo DaVinci's sketches, for engineers to figure out how to leverage air pressure to create enough lift to detach humans from the ground. More recently, you only have to look at the last thirty years that have been dedicated to recreate the mythic hoverboard that appeared in the movie *Back to the Future*, some attempts getting very close to reality (Wikipedia HoverBoard Entry, s.d.). If it is deemed impossible, it should probably better be phrased as "not obviously possible at the moment".

The most important aspect of innovation is inspiration. A great idea or vision is not bothered by feasibility the same way that airplanes or hoverboards are not anchored by gravity. To look for inspiration, remember that nothing is out of reach. Look for improvements opportunities and reflect on the goals you want to accomplish to shape your vision. The feasibility will eventually transform this vision to bend itself to the laws of nature, but your vision must remain true to its goals, it is based on "going where no one has gone before". End of science-fiction theme.

Let's meet at the next crossroad

We have established that anything is possible as long as you apply enough time and resources. Given this law, you must probably ask yourself how to translate this into real world projects, especially considering that modern organizations are made of many departments and structures with a diversity of priorities and processes. And of course, you do not dispose of infinite time and resources. Despite this fragmentation of management, something

NO MATTER WHAT PEOPLE TELL YOU, WORDS AND IDEAS CAN CHANGE THE WORLD. - ROBIN WILLIAMS

remains as part of the unicity of the organization: the overall goals that are defined in the mission of the business. These goals and the strategies that are in motion to achieve them should be common to all aspects of the enterprise; they are the glue that ensures that you are dedicating efforts geared towards achieving them.

This is how the efforts and the time can be variations even inside your organization. Think of it like a nation going into battle. The goal is to win the war but not every cavalry or infantry division will attack the enemy directly; some may be used at the flanks, others used to spread the enemy's resources and others, unfortunately, may be sacrificed to create strategic opportunities. These are all tactical behaviours that, while very different in their limited objectives, work towards a common strategic goal. This is the main difference between being strategic or tactical.

A strategy is common to the entire structure of the organization because it drives a common goal. The organization's divisions, whether they be geographical, political or otherwise, may adapt their execution differently in order to achieve this common goal, which is a tactical decision that is managed by the division but ultimately approved by the strategic council. The strategy's focus is the end result while the tactical focus deals with the process milestone; many different processes can work together or meet the needs to reach the same results. The strategic council is there to orchestrate the tactical maneuvers to guarantee maximum effectiveness.

Chapter Summary

Do not overthink what you need to do or how to do it to achieve a specific goal. At the inspiration stage, you must focus on the vision to inspire and motivate. Let the people in your organization contribute to the vision by completing the dots, they will provide the tactical details to the strategy. In fact, as mentioned in this chapter, your organization's divisions may take completely different roads to reach this common goal and that will make the journey so much more fruitful.

SET YOUR GOALS HIGH, AND DON'T STOP TILL YOU GET THERE. - BO JACKSON

Part 2 - The shortcut to far, far away

"After much consideration, testing out how it floats on a model first sounds great..."

Summary

Start questioning everything you know about your business. In the second part, the common theme will be about learning something new and trying things out instead of planning everything in advance, because mistakes and failures are the path to wisdom. That way, you will learn more about what you CAN do (you never really know until you try pushing your limits) and discover the customer's deep desires from their point of view. Most of these unspoken or unrevealed needs are so deeply rooted that people often forget about them. The opportunity is everywhere, but you have to be able to see them for what they are.

Chapter 4 – The science of introspection: know thyself

Topics covered

In this chapter, we will focus on uncovering opportunities that are oblivious to most people. We will do this by asking questions in a very different way, surfacing the actual need that customers overlook and getting to know people in ways that they haven't realized themselves. Digging to the root of the problem and providing an answer that is fresh and different is the key to innovate and leapfrog competitors.

A bit of history

You may have heard the expression "*know thyself*", which is often attributed to the Greek philosopher Socrates in the works of Plato. In fact, it is probably much more ancient that this, having appeared in monuments writings as early as those of the Luxor Temple in Egypt. It refers to the arduous work of studying oneself and to understand better why we do the things we do. Even though it could cover many books (and it has), innovation is not about knowing yourself but about knowing ourselves as a people. To be aware and understand the issues that face us every day as consumers is key to developing great inspiration that target great customer experiences. The modern approach to great business acumen is all about empathy.

It's easier said than done because it's about delivering to people what they need instead of delivering what they want or is expected. For instance, if Henry Ford would have asked his customers what they wanted, they would have probably said a faster or lighter horse carriage. If you haven't noticed, most customers asking a question like this will answer with the solution they are familiar with and expect, not a result or goal they hope to achieve. What they obviously really wanted was to get to their destination faster and more efficiently. Of course, had he listened to his customers literally, he would have never invented a car because his customers could not yet have expressed their goals in these words.

Another good example of overriding a customer's request with the customer's goal happened with Apple's introduction of the original iMac.

TO KNOW ONESELF, ONE SHOULD ASSERT ONESELF. - ALBERT CAMUS

Back then, Apple took the bold decision to eliminate the floppy drive which was the industry standard way of saving files at the time. This aggravated just about everyone because old reliable technology was now obsolete. The industry was shaking its head, trying to understand what Apple was trying to do, especially since this was the same company that popularized this exact floppy format more than a decade before. But if customers were asking for a floppy drive, what they were actually hoping for was simple information exchange. Apple instead opted for network-based data exchange with an integrated modem and ethernet network card. Apple also decided to bet on a new technology that aimed to be simpler and more reliable than the floppy drive, the Universal Serial Bus (USB).

This was a courageous bet and a dangerous one. Customers might have chosen to change systems rather than contemplate changing all their ways. The company was betting on two basic principles: people love convenience over old impractical ways and Moore's Law. The latter one defines that the number of transistors in a circuit doubles every two years, which means that any USB-based flash memory storage would quickly grow in capacity faster than the floppy, making large files easier to manage with USB storage or through network transfers. Undoubtedly, it is much easier to react to customers' requests than to anticipate their true goals; the secret sauce of potent innovation is to ask the question that bypasses the customer's solution in favor of the customer's wish list.

The missing link and the archaeologist

Field work is grueling, but nobody can deny that it is rarely unfulfilling. There is no substitute for living the moment; you can do all the surveys you want, and you will never be able to capture all the intricate details of the user experience unless you live them yourself. There is no way to design a set of questions that will cover all aspects of this situation, nor is there a way for a writer to describe a scene so perfectly in a book that it can be recreated twice the same way in a movie. Archaeologists often travel to the site of the subject of their research to get a first account accurate perspective of the ancient people's environment.

GET GOOD COUNSEL BEFORE YOU BEGIN: AND WHEN YOU HAVE DECIDED, ACT PROMPTLY. - SALLUST

AmuseD by Innovation

To use a product or service exposes the innovator to realities that might not have been visible otherwise. One does not invent a microwave oven by improving on the heating elements of conventional ovens: they search for a way to cook food faster. The conventional oven might work adequately but repeated use makes it clear that it requires more planning and time allocation, which has been disappearing steadily with a modern lifestyle. Because there is a need for a better oven, research must turn to faster methods that go beyond heating elements, to discover that exciting the molecules of food under a strong microwave emitter can generate heat inside the food, thus cooking in minutes instead of hours. The innovation must take its inspiration from goals that improve the result, which leads to research and discoveries that attack the source of the problem.

With field experience, if you are diligent, you can even uncover needs that clients are not aware of and develop solutions that are completely unexpected, crossing into the realm of transnovation with products or services that are in a class of their own without equivalent.

For example, to this day, I still don't know why I do not have something that automatically flosses and brushes my teeth after every meal even though my dentist tells me I need to. Where is the transnovation breakthrough that will change my life forever? Life tends to run in a straight line, and we don't question many things that we take for granted; we live on autopilot and have come to accept it. In innovation, complacency is opportunity.

Ask the oracle

If inspiration to innovate requires a level of customer insight that goes beyond the customer's initial desires, then how can you scratch beyond the surface? The answer relies in asking the correct question. The question should have been: what are you trying to achieve, what does success and satisfaction looks like to you? If you could envision anything, what would be on your wish list? Your perfect answer would have been "I don't know the solution to this riddle but now that I know what to aim for, I can iterate and explore options that will reach these results in the closest way possible".

I LEARN BY GOING WHERE I HAVE TO GO. - THEODORE ROETHKE

Chapter Summary

Inspiration to innovate can be challenging since it needs to craft a vision that goes beyond what customers, or your competition, expects. This requires a very special skill set in asking the right question to not necessarily deliver what customers request but what they should be provided to reach an unprecedented level of delight. You must master the art of asking the right question. Do not ask: "how can I give you what you want" or "how to make an experience better". This assumes that your customer knows the answer. Ask your customer: "what is in your wish list, how can I create an experience beyond your expectations?"

YOU CREATE YOUR OPPORTUNITIES BY ASKING FOR THEM. - SHAKTI GAWAIN

Chapter 5 – Breaking the mold is only the beginning

Topics covered

In this chapter, we will look at the disruptive forces that can influence your innovation agenda: they can be the agents of change, or they can alter the course of your project timeline. Disruption used to be about natural or unpredictable circumstances, but the modern world is a disruptive universe in perpetual turmoil. In this chapter, we will discover that the organizations that will master the art of surfing and taking advantage of these relentless transformations will come out on top.

A bit of history

Disruption happens when an unforeseen event is introduced that breaks the normal flow of activities. In the past, these disruptions were often associated with natural disasters, which had huge repercussions due to the immense amount of energy that is released by earthquakes, tornadoes, hurricanes, volcanoes and so on. Not until human mastered the atom has there been enough power from man-made activities to generate such levels of disruption in so little time.

These natural disasters are unfortunately often tragic due to inadequate forethought from urban planning, resulting in an enormous loss of life and economic damage. This was the case in the famous 1906 San Francisco earthquake, where city officials avoided the word "earthquake" and downplayed the number of casualties to avoid the fleeing of investors looking to rebuild (San Francisco 1906 Earthquake, s.d.). While questionable, this strategy proved to be ultimately successful as the city was mostly rebuilt by 1915. One of the most important disasters of the last century in the United States with over three thousand lives lost, it contributed to the awareness of implementing countermeasures for earthquakes such as the development of building earthquake dampers and other preventive technologies.

What history teaches us is that the most disruptive the event is, the more widespread is the change. This is true as well for any major technology

---

BECAUSE THINGS ARE THE WAY THEY ARE, THINGS WILL NOT STAY THE WAY THEY ARE. - BERTOLT BRECHT changes that creates deep social transformations. Also, it is interesting to note that just like aftershocks happen with earthquakes, major technology changes send ripples of aftershocks long after they are introduced.

A good example of this is the introduction of the camera on the cell phone. Not only did this create a change of habit with users, who now were able to capture any moment at any time because of their constant access to a camera, but it had significant repercussions long after that affected many other social activities and industries. For instance, the analog photography film and reflex camera industry along with the video camera industry started plummeting soon after. The businesses specializing in the photography development needed to transform first as printing bureaus and soon could not adapt to the shift to virtual photos cyber walls that instantly share with friends. This even prompted new policies into the management of public areas now that anyone could send to the Internet any footage instantly, including disturbing behavior from public authorities.

Indeed, the most disruptive the event is, the more it needs to be revisited because not only can it have major repercussions in the customer lifestyle, but it can also have social aftershocks long past its initial disruption.

Survival of the fittest

Having established that external events can be disruptive, it is essential that your organization stays sensitized to special needs that can arise from these unforeseen circumstances. However, how can we handle disruption that was planned? What we are talking about here is a situation where the event is purposely engineered to create a new iconic moment in time for which someone ends up being on the reactive side? As you may have guessed, it's always preferable to be on the initiator side than on the reactive side.

Disruption can also be a strategic event that is targeted at initiating and capturing a customer's attention by introducing a new experience that diverges significantly from the old. Many small companies have successfully used this technique to displace large established organizations, taking advantage of simultaneous events that impose a change of habits. Based on

---

THE WORLD HATES CHANGE, YET IT IS THE ONLY THING THAT HAS BROUGHT PROGRESS. - CHARLES F. KETTERING

AmuseD by Innovation

the fact that the world is constantly changing, smaller organizations are more naturally nimble and can adapt quickly to exterior forces. Just like natural evolution, the ones who survive do not require a lot of resources and usually thrive with change: they constantly analyze customers being much closer to them and deliver that next step of experience because their risk is minimal, they have nothing to lose!

A great example is that, not so long ago, the Internet was big enough to require tools for users to locate information but small enough that it could be organized. In many ways, it was used very much like a phone book, a directory of useful addresses indexed in a consumable fashion that was familiar to most people. This developed into the Internet catalogs of that era such as Yahoo, America Online and Alta Vista. Yet, the Internet was growing too fast for anyone to effectively track its information, so fast in fact that only the combined power of all Internet users could index it all. A small company decided to put all this power to good use, enriching tracking engines exponentially, to develop into the most successful search engine on the planet and now a synonym for retrieving information: Google.

Disruption can be a planned event based on the transformation of the world around us; the organization that can tap into these transformations efficiently and produce innovation that answers these new requirements can generate a tsunami and reset the world to its clock.

Let's play Follow the leader

Clearly, the best place to be is on the disruptive side of the balance. Knowing that innovation takes time to develop, the reactive mode creates an opportunity for smaller more agile organizations that have been studying your customers for a sizeable amount of time to move in your territory. That strategy is most often designed for maximum effectiveness, with innovations that take a lot of effort, purposely built to make your product or service look ancient and misguided. By the time you can react, it is often too late.

Why wait to be disrupted? Instead, invest today to challenge yourself! Think of this like an organization that creates a hostile force within, to simulate a

I DWELL IN POSSIBILITY. - EMILY DICKINSON

real threat. Microsoft tests on a regular basis their own security measures using a blue and red team. The idea is to actively thwart the other team's security to find the holes in their systems in order to patch them accordingly. Implement something similar in your organization: a hostile small agile business that can challenge your traditional model with innovative ideas and your business culture. You may find that you will gain from learning your weaknesses yourself instead of waiting for someone else to do it for you – at your expense.

One does not need to wait for disruption to happen in a damaging way; you may prefer to trigger it and lead it, forcing others to follow in your footsteps thus leading the new wave of innovation with your name, actions and reputation.

Challenge yourself before someone else does

I opened this book with the importance of innovation in today's business strategy for growth and survival. I did point out that you may find me alarmist, maybe you do not feel threatened in your market or industry. If you wonder why I often start my chapters with little stories, it's because I am convinced that history tends to repeat itself. If you are a student of history, you can learn a lot from past mistakes and at the very least try to avoid those.

In the past, many other organizations felt that they were at the top of their power and expected to remain there for the foreseeable future. Then, disruption came along in the form of a small technology breakthrough that those large institutions did not pay enough attention to, resulting in very costly mistakes. I would like to recall to this readership a few classic historic mistakes that ended in obliterating the establishment. One needs only to think about the discovery of a small compound called gun powder, the microchip and the personal computer that displaced the mainframe, software transactions by volume instead of big packages in the form of Apple micro-transactions (often 99 cents per app, or freemium (Freemium, s.d.)) offered to mobility devices that now represent more than ten times the amount of personal computers.

ARRIVING AT ONE GOAL IS THE STARTING POINT TO ANOTHER. - JOHN DEWEY

AmuseD by Innovation

There are hard lessons to be learned from these events. Frequently, outside external circumstances are the triggers that force this awakening to innovative customer experiences. Often, it is near fatal for the reactive parties until the new crowned leader becomes large enough itself and slows down its innovation, to be challenged by newcomers. The secret is to look behind to glimpse at the competition ganging up while looking forward to the next wave. And compete as if you were the disruptor.

Get some fashion-sense

There is an industry out there that looks remarkably like the generalized competing trends in all markets today: the fashion world. While I do not pretend to know anything about fashion (I am colour blind, which makes me handicapped right from the start), I have always been fascinated by the way it is so competitive.

The fashion industry is constantly keeping an eye on trends. It tries to predict the future, one season at a time, by analyzing what is hot, what is not, what the world is morphing into. It tries to shape those trends by listening to the giants of the Haute Couture yet remains highly aware of the emerging trends and challengers of the fashion world. It is extremely well informed about history and the past styles to measure the new currents against the old designs. Finally, it keeps tabs on what is being done inside their competitors' community and makes sure that nothing is quite comparable to them in one form or another.

Trends spotting is like the fashion world. Due to the acceleration of changes brought upon by new easily accessible technologies such as the cloud, 3D printing and other tools, it is increasingly becoming evident that trends are more elusive than ever. If you know your environment as well as a fashion designer, your brand will be and will remain the trend-setter.

Chapter Summary

Be on the lookout for the changes occurring around you and the pretenders looking for a piece of the pie. They may not have your resources and experience but do not discard them; they are likely not going to attack your business the same way you would and may give you a ride for your money. They are ready to start fresh; they are listening to the needs of the current customer and to the movements of the environment. Make sure to position yourself as the trend-setter by creating teams that challenge themselves inside your organization with the same level of rivalry that your competition would show you to create a challenging innovation agenda.

AmuseD by Innovation

Chapter 6 – Learn to play and play to learn

Topics covered

In this chapter, we will revisit a concept we hinted at earlier, the human capacity for change. Many innovations, while perfectly conceived and immensely useful, have failed because it was just not the right time. Humans are notorious for being creatures that find comfort in predictable environments. For this reason, managing the speed of today's acceleration of change should be part of everyone's priority. This chapter explains how to handle this major obstacle course. Spoiler alert: the solution is not to remove humans from the equation.

A bit of history

Years ago, my eldest boy came to me needing help with his studies. I was raised in a small town with nothing much to do except hockey (which I am not very keen on, making me an outcast compared to the average French Canadian). By far, my favorite past time was reading, and, like my older sibling, I grew to become an intellectual. The world in 2016 is very different; kids are now bombarded with the Internet, cell phone chats, social networks, gaming and so on: plenty of distractions to keep you from focusing. For this reason, my son, like a lot of kids, was having difficulty learning an abstract topic that requires a hefty dose of concentration: algebra.

I was trying desperately to help him understand the concept of containers and operations when I realized something: the problem was not about what I was explaining but how I was doing it. His method of learning was quite different than my own. I enjoy drawing and building stuff and can abstract concepts easily without seeing them at the physical level, something my son was struggling with. And so, I changed my method by illustrating concepts such as multiplications (groups), divisions (partitions) and subtractions (debts). By demonstrating that when you have a debt of 5 things – no matter what they are -- and I ask you to remove 3 more things from your possessions (that you do not have), I clearly put you in a state with a debt of 8 things to give back to re-establish a debt free status. Suddenly, my son understood

---

BEGIN TO BE NOW WHAT YOU WILL BE HEREAFTER. - WILLIAM JAMES

that he did not need to know the nature of the things to acquire an additional debt, the same as the addition of a subtraction event.

What this made me recognize is that while everybody can learn, not everybody learns the same way. We need to adjust our teaching and learning techniques by developing them to be adaptable, often by letting the students discover on their own, the best way to assimilate knowledge. This is a lifetime skill. Therefore, we all need to learn about learning the best way to learn. Yeah, it's a mind twister...

The deep side of the pool with floaters

The main issue with learning new things is that there is fear of failing. At the same time, as you learn more, your apprehension of discovering and trying new bolder experiences become less severe. Since innovation is based solely on new concepts that are unfamiliar and, purposely, out of your comfort zone, one can anticipate the challenge of receiving enthusiastic participation in such a risky dreadful endeavor. How do you make this less scary and more attractive?

Think of it as if you did not know how to swim but are required to go the deep end of the pool. If you are not scared, there is something seriously wrong with you. However, if you are provided with all the means to protect yourself, using floaters, a pole to hang on to, even the friendly hand of a trusted companion, then that fear is alleviated and you are much more confident in trying out that adventure, despite the fact that between the ground and your feet will be nothing else but a few meters of water. This is because you are given assurance that if something goes wrong, you will not drown and get help right away. Jumping into innovation for newcomers is a lot like jumping in the deep end of the pool.

Innovation is scary only if you don't have all the protection you need: this is in the form of ensuring that there is help available if you need it and also by having enough knowledge about the environment to feel confident that if something goes wrong, you will be alright. Knowledge assimilated from a new environment is quite effective at calming fears because you forget

YOU CAN'T CROSS THE SEA MERELY BY STANDING AND STARING AT THE WATER. - RABINDRANATH TAGORE

AmuseD by Innovation

danger after having done something new long enough. It's like riding a bike: you forget the risk of falling when you ride it often enough because you have done this many times and feel confident that you will not fall.

I strongly encourage organizations that aspire to innovate to let their employees play with new technologies to let it sink in, to create familiarity with them. Play time is learning the most you can about something new so that it has no more secret -- and thus is not that scary anymore. So go ahead and try new things to learn from them. PLAY TIME!

Build it and they will come

There is one more reason why learning by trial is essential. First-hand experience provides a unique perspective that can help you develop intuition, which is just another word for the capacity of the human brain to infer knowledge from observations. This process can save huge amounts of effort by letting individuals bypass certain paths of development that intuitively do not "feel" as promising as others and try out ones that give you more confidence. This is a direct opposite to what has been taught in science since time immemorial; the recommended approach is usually to infer next steps from a lot of observations and develop a hypothesis that can be verified.

While this is commendable and definitely required in some fields, I cannot stress more the fact that innovation is accelerating and that time is of the essence. Trust your judgement to give you the insight to take the path of least resistance.

I am not quite sure if the story I share with you now is folklore or a true scientific study, but it probably holds some truth. The story goes like this: a competition is equally initiated with engineers and children to find the fastest method to hold an egg using a structure built with toothpicks. As you might have guessed, the story goes on to explain how the kids won the competition over the engineers. The reason is quite simple; while the engineers debated on the most efficient way of building the structure, making it strong and resilient, the kids knew nothing of the sort but instead

YOU MUST DO THE THINGS YOU THINK YOU CANNOT DO. - ELEANOR ROOSEVELT tried many different iterations until they started identifying a pattern that worked and enriched it quickly. The engineers failed because they spent all their time analyzing without really knowing what to expect from the toothpicks' properties. The kids did not know anything but learned through trial and error what works and what doesn't (learning about toothpicks). Their prototype, while not perfect, achieved the goal of the experiment.

Undeniably, the engineers would have found the best method based on very solid and verifiable calculations. The amount of effort and time, however, would have most likely been greater. The moral of this story is that prototyping is not a process that replaces the scientific method but rather a way of identifying faster elementary concepts that accelerate the initial inspiration into a minimum viable product (MVP), which will later be refined by a more formal process.

Prototyping is a very efficient way to learn quickly key concepts that can be applied towards a more structured goal. Sometimes, it just helps to build without really planning it (winging it), in a frugal and scaled down approach, to learn the maximum amount of experimental data in the shortest amount of time. Of course, if you have access to historic data from past similar experiments, it definitely helps but it does not replace your personal learning exercise. This is where experience outplays knowledge.

Keep up the good work

Everybody is different. Technology is evolving at a wild pace. Finding the right skills is getting harder every day. Despite all the tools and help you implement; you seem to always fall behind. This is starting to feel like a battle you cannot win. Take comfort at least in the thought that you are not alone.

Schools are struggling with our children as well. The old ways of teaching are not working anymore. Peoples' abilities to learn are in transition and the tools to support this change are still scarce. It would greatly please me to tell you that there is a miracle solution to fix everything, but I think we have a long way to go to find it. Maybe artificial intelligence will figure out our flaws in the future and work around them but this moment has not arrived yet.

THERE IS NOTHING IMPOSSIBLE TO HIM WHO WILL TRY. - ALEXANDER THE GREAT

AmuseD by Innovation

What I do want to mention is the fact that the human learning evolution is one of the hottest topics in research today.

To appreciate the complexity of such a colossal undertaking, we need to take a step back and look at how we developed knowledge assimilation in the past. First, we started by developing schools to teach to others; that was the first order of learning that I will label "L1". Then, we looked at how to teach better to learn in a more efficient method, which is also called pedagogy; I will label this "L2". But pedagogy is hitting a wall with the human capacity to absorb the amount of information that is needed as we go forward. The mathematics that was taught in college thirty years ago are now being taught at the high school level to make way for more current teachings in college. Worst, they are fighting with other science skills for this limited amount of time that children can dedicate to learning. What has been happening to schools in the last decades is now transposing in the workforce; nobody can keep up.

This is the realm of metacognition, what I label "L3". Metacognition is defined as *"awareness or analysis of one's own learning or thinking processes"* (Metacognition, s.d.). It is becoming ever more evident that we must introduce modern thinking into the processes used to train people to pick up knowledge faster. Organizations must become more involved into all three learning levels (the three Ls): learning, learning to learn better and finally learning about how we can improve our processes of better learning. I apologize for this headache; it just emphasizes my point about our human limitations to assimilate concepts.

Chapter Summary

Few can achieve innovation by jumping in the deep end when you don't know how to swim. The truth is that many will drown that way. Adapting to an innovation agenda is a gradual process through which, the innovator becomes progressively familiar with the new technologies and tries new ways to explore them, always daring to go a bit further, a bit deeper. Exploration and play time are part of the fabric of modern learning by actively testing new methods and extrapolate the results based on previous experiments. This is one of many ways the learning process is evolving, and leading-edge organizations should pay close attention to the developments in this field. Experimentation and modern knowledge sharing techniques help redefine the ideation process essential to innovation.

ONE FINDS LIMITS BY PUSHING THEM. - HERBERT SIMON

Part 3 – Cockroaches and entropy

About 250 million years ago: "All your mother and I are saying is that this newfound fur of yours might not be the best way to fit in..."

Summary

At the end of the world, only two things will still be around – cockroaches and entropy. Cockroaches are a given and change is inevitable; as you embrace it, you need to equip yourself to adopt this new world as your own. Part 3 is most definitely the part of the book you have been waiting for, what I have been preparing you for, since chapter 1.

This is the part that will start to assemble the components of every innovation agenda into manageable answers. This part will also provide a set of contemporary technology concepts that can be applied as building blocks for your innovation agenda, seeding the much-needed inspiration process. I will help you define the key questions of the "**who**", the "**what**", the "**how**", the "**where**" and the "**when**" that are all critical to preparing your innovation agenda. Jump in, the water's fine.

Chapter 7 – Carving stairs in the mountain

Topics covered

In this chapter, I will share with you my framework to generate innovation ideas. As stated in the early pages of this book, in order to launch an innovation agenda, inspiration is one of the hardest challenges to overcome. This methodology, developed to help you achieve small successes to reach a greater goal, will ignite opportunities of innovation that you can later develop into your own fully fleshed ideas, branded with your unique style and experience. It will align your key objectives to modern technology trends and help you specify strategic components to let you concentrate on the tactical aspects afterwards.

A bit of history

Now that we are at the point in the book where we start talking about generating inspiration for innovation, we can now panic in front of the blank page. Where do we start? This seems like a task for Hercules, an undertaking worthy of a demigod in the same league as moving a mountain.

This reminds me of a meeting I had a while back, geared towards migrating traditionally locally installed applications to the cloud. To say that my client was reluctant would be an understatement; my client was sceptic that we could tackle this beast of a project. So, I decided to give in to the vision and picture this beast the same way they did, like climbing a mountain. Difficult and risky. Then, I switched my presentation to a Mexican pyramid of similar size but with the major difference that tourists were climbing its stairs. My point was that we could tackle this "mountain" by carving stairs in it, climbing one step at a time. In other words, I was suggesting breaking this mega project into manageable chunks and to start with baby steps. They followed this with "what do you suggest"? I smiled and went on for almost an hour with very attentive people listening to every detail of my proposal. The roadmap was set and I had sculpted the first step with a general idea of where we would be going next.

IMAGINATION IS MORE IMPORTANT THAN KNOWLEDGE. - ALBERT EINSTEIN

AmuseD by Innovation

Years later, I learned that steps in mountains is a common thing in China so you may want to use this instead in the future. The image is quite striking, and the message cannot be clearer: anything hard or seemingly unsurmountable can be made possible if only you build manageable steps to get to the end point.

Make me one with everything

Like a classic joke (and a favorite one of mine) from the late Robin Williams, the story goes like this: *"what does the yogi asks at the hot dog stand? – Make me one with everything!"* If the hot dog is the answer to everything, then this explains why we haven't figured it out yet. Depending on your point of view, every complex answer requires many questions. Developing an inspiration for innovation is right up there. One of these questions has been answered; we have extensively iterated the importance of an innovation agenda and can safely say that the "why" part of our checklist is done. The next items on the list will be addressed in the following pages.

The secret to structuring a solid business case for an innovation project is no different than any other project: proper planning. The most important difference is by far that TIME is working against you. Time is relevant when it comes to getting access to key technology, methods and resources. Time also affects the suitability of the innovation, as there is such a thing as being ahead of your time or too late.

A good innovation project must deal with key questions early on:

- what are we trying to achieve (the goal).
- where are we going to concentrate our effort and energy.
- when are we planning to deliver a prototype or a working offering.
- who is the primary target to consume this product/service.
- how can be deliver the best product/service in the most efficient manner possible.

Ultimate simulation: let's hit 88 mph!

The cards system I developed is purposely built in a way that can answer these questions in the most logical way possible. If you have a goal ("why" you need innovation), you should be able to state the technology advancement that you wish to tap into to inject innovation (the "how" you will transform your product or service) and start to define an early sketch of the innovation project that will address this goal (as in "what is the innovation that you want to implement"). Try this out with a simple simulation, as if you were in the future.

If you can state a possible technology advancement that was instrumental in addressing your goal as a fictitious futuristic case study, you can easily test how this innovation sounds. Try to see if you can use this hypothesis and write something along those lines to test it out: "My company X needed to improve A (why: goal, need) for the benefits of our target clientele (who). Taking advantage of our innovative approach Y (what: the innovation) applied with the following methods and tools Z (how: methods & resources) to these specific areas of the business (where), we were able to achieve this goal just in time with the perfectly orchestrated assistance from our people (when)."

Chapter Summary

This chapter is the entry into Part 3 and is the most critical part of your innovation agenda planning; this is why it is the biggest section in the book. If you have multiple ideas (and you should brainstorm to get a lot of those), making a table that defines the why, where, when, who and how will go a long way towards defining the what and the metrics that will guide you into reviewing the best ROI for each one of your innovation ideas, to prioritize the ones that are the most valuable and strategic to your business.

YOU WILL NEVER WIN IF YOU NEVER BEGIN. - HELEN ROWLAND

AmuseD by Innovation

Chapter 8 – Meditate the meaning of Life

Topics covered

In this chapter, we will work at defining the scope and the impact of your innovation agenda. This is really more a suggested approach rather than a prescriptive part of the process. The reason is that, within the innovation development timeline, you may want to change the scope or even possibly calibrate the impact that you wish to generate from this innovation. We mentioned that innovating takes time and that you need to remain flexible during this progress since many changes can occur, internal or external, that will force you to deviate from your initial plan. We will show how to keep the goal steady yet allow the project to alter its course gracefully.

A bit of history

Earlier in the book, I explained why my understanding of innovation is something defined within a product or service line and why I named the introduction of a completely new product or service class a "transnovation". I strongly suspect this comes from my years of Kung Fu training; I tend to view the world as internal styles and external styles (Chinese Martial Arts External and Internal classifications, s.d.). In that sense, innovation is very much based on the strengths that you already have as part of your expertise while "transnovation" is in a category on its own, without the burden of legacy. In that sense, "transnovation" is external since it is turned towards a brand-new experience, ready to be shaped by the customers' feedbacks.

Both hold the potential for success within your organization, but their strategic importance is very different. Take the story of Jeff Bezos' Amazon. The mission statement of Amazon is *"to be earth's most customer-centric company; to build a place where people can come to find and discover anything they might want to buy online."* While Amazon's shares have been trading at a record high in the last few years, it was not the top performer that it is today for quite a while. If you ask investors, they will probably tell you that it never pays back dividends (Stocks without dividends, s.d.). This is because Amazon is most definitely a hybrid innovation/"transnovation"

SHOOT FOR THE MOON AND IF YOU MISS YOU WILL STILL BE AMONG THE STARS. - LES BROWN

company; it constantly reinvests its gains in improving its service lines as well as creating new ventures and markets to expand its influence.

It's important to decide early what kind of impact you hope to achieve from your innovation agenda. "Transnovation" involves more risk and will cost more in R&D; it will also probably require a hefty investment in market research and product/service publicity to create customer awareness. Amazon did not turn a profit for a very long time when it launched but its market strategy eventually paid off, starving a lot of smaller businesses using extremely low margins for such a huge organization. This turned Amazon into the powerhouse that it is today with a market share that is unique amongst both online and brick & mortar retailers. Innovation on an existing product or service can at least leverage a current customer base and a level of awareness but will usually not generate as much attention.

The right angle to every circle

This is not to say that one cannot transform into the other. There are many cases where an existing product or service went on to introduce such an important amount of innovation in one generation that it forked into a whole new line. One only has to think about how Apple originally introduced the iPhone to the world. They already had the established iPod line as a media player and had history with Internet-enabled devices like the iMac. When Steve Jobs came on stage, he announced that Apple was introducing three revolutionary products: *"...an iPod, a phone and an Internet communicator (...) are you getting it? These are not three separate devices, this is one device and we are calling it iPhone!"* Apple took the venerable iPod and gave it communication capabilities that were such a departure that it gave birth to a new product line, a "transnovation".

Even though you may look at a product or service evolution as a cycle of iterations, there may be situations where a few babies will be "different" and deserve a classification of their own.

So, despite the fact that you will need to identify the "what" of your innovation agenda to align with your business strategy and investments, do not be surprised if the "what" changes shape during its maturity cycle. Babies look the same in a nursery but grow up completely different.

As a rule of thumb, if you choose to create a "splash" with a "transnovation", you will need to address the following in terms of additional effort:

- Pay attention to clients' social transformations, not just their current consumption of products/services.
- Take into consideration a longer ramp-up to make people aware of the product or service, understand its value proposition and allocate time to convince them.
- Expect a longer time to gain an ROI but, if the "transnovation" is a success, it will be a clear advantage over the competition and will require massive resources to secure the market quickly.

Be sure to leverage many concepts from past innovation brainstorming sessions to help customers realize how different this new offering is, from what you did in the past or anything else on the market. Make tactical use of your strengths to reduce your R&D cycle and insert virtual building blocks, placeholders for unidentified technologies, where your vision cannot yet attach specific solutions. The development of a successful "transnovation" project requires a social stethoscope that can pinpoint trends and track them down to the source of that social evolution, so that it can transcend the current unpolished desire and carve the diamond that is the sharp vision that you want to promote. A "transnovation" is a transformative agent, with a deeper meaning.

Namaste to you too

As you can see, innovation often deals with a clear future, a normal evolution of a current product or service. The way of "transnovation" is quite different, betting on an uncertain future that is malleable, that can still be shaped by the unique "greatness" that your vision provides. I say "Namaste" to you, if you choose to take that road; I bow to your greatness, it is obviously inspired by the muses. You have managed to listen to your customers and gain a level

---

A GOAL IS A DREAM WITH A DEADLINE. - NAPOLEON HILL

of unparalleled insight that not only captures their current needs but also envisions where these needs will evolve through internal and external forces. To be able to mine the customer's progress in a way that you can forecast its evolution in time is to reach total enlightenment of your market, innovation Nirvana (Nirvana, s.d.).

To make an impact with innovation, it is essential that you ask yourself, "What do I want to be" and be inspired to generate the innovations that will help define what you want to be. Avoid the questions like "What do I need to do" because this is a question about "how" to do it and this will come later. Be purposeful. Guy Kawasaki calls this your mantra.

Mature to realize your mantra

At a TEDx presentation in Berkeley (TEDx Berkeley Guy Kawasaki, s.d.), the Apple alumni Guy Kawasaki explained the important difference between an organization's mission and its mantra. I will try to capture his thoughts: he proposes that the mantra is a set of a few words that define why your meaning should exist. By meaning, he wishes an organization to clearly state what its purpose in life is, what you want to contribute to the world and why you should exist. If you're a company, you obviously want to be successful, but this is not your mantra; the mantra is your unique contribution that will make or break your success. The mantra is ultimately short, but your mission statement relates more the "how" of achieving your vision, talking about the values that you promote in your organization to flesh out your mantra.

My personal mantra is "help others to make a better world". This is why I believe my contribution, as small as it is, has a purpose and this is why I love what I do. Because I work at realizing my mantra every day, my purpose is clear; how can I not be successful if I do a good job at helping others be better?

With a mantra, your path is obvious. Determined, your vision of where you want to go is more defined. Recognizing what you know and what you do not know, you can structure an overall strategy. It should include what you envision as part of your innovation roadmap that can improve what you do or start something completely new.

Chapter Summary

The "what" question can easily turn into a "how" question, at which point your innovation agenda can transform itself into a standard improvement project. If you clarify your unique contribution to the world, your mantra acts as a filter to compel you to introduce ideas that contribute to realize yourself. From this point on, the impact you wish to have is a matter of defining how this inspired vision can serve your strategy. You may not be another Steve Jobs, but you are given the chance to shape the future with your dream, and it is up to you to see how far you want to take it.

Chapter 9 – Location, location, location...

Topics covered

In this chapter, we tackle the infamous "where" question; one with a broad scope since it can be applied in many parts of your innovation agenda. We will review the implications of executing specific phases of your project in particular locations and the processes adjustments that can be expected. Also, we will consider where to apply modern capabilities that impact this form of project management to increase your return on investment.

A bit of history

In the introduction, we alluded to the era of the machine, a somewhat scary and even taboo subject. Nevertheless, we are facing this revolution, and it accomplishes nothing to bury your head in the sand; you need to meet this head on. It may surprise you that this is a bigger concern in countries that heavily rely on manufacturing than countries that are services oriented. This is because we are on the verge of an efficiency rapture: humans and animals are no longer a logical commodity for many jobs, including the ones that used to depend on higher brain functions such as physical perception or decision-making.

Many of the traditional manufacturing countries such as China (you know, made in China...) are seeing the ubiquitous robot as a true economic threat, which urges them to invest massively into restructuring their workforce for the coming times. These countries are building power plants to feed the huge amounts of energy that will be required to sustain this economic transformation. We have reached a point where building offshore and transporting finished goods is costing more than using local robots.

The reason is simple: the dumb robot is going the way of the dodo. Modern robots and artificial intelligence, paired with cheap sensors and actuators, are now competing with human efficiency, no matter where you are on the globe. In some cases, they are winning the game due to the fact that they are relentless and don't require salaries, just energy, parts and maintenance. This changes the global economic dynamics since a robot in an offshore

AmuseD by Innovation

country does not cost much more than a domestic robot, factoring the recurring cost of the transportation of goods against the higher wages or maintenance in non-manufacturing countries. This "where" question is now morphing from a location in the globe to a question about where to invest the next generation of automation.

Let's play "Where's Waldo?"

Given that the dynamics of resource allocation are changing considerably, the "where" question, be it that its nature is highly tactical, becomes very important to improve the innovation project's profitability. Just like real estate, it's all about location, location, location.

You need to identify three key areas of your innovation plan:

- **where should I invest time and expenses** to improve my processes (phases breakdown): this relates to the methods (automation) that you wish to use, that will influence the other decisions.
- **where can I find the best work resources** to achieve my goal (people or machines): this is about deciding on workforce provisioning, based on the approach selected (which can be traditional or automated);
- **where should I locate the specific components of the project** to provide me the attributes that I need (location): this relates to the global positioning of the specific tasks (costs reduction, climate or environmental propensity, distance from distribution, etc.)

All three "where" questions have many more subparts, which we will not dive into because of space constraints. Suffice it to say that the devil is in the details. Many of these scenarios can also be combined to support a whole spectrum of new delivery capabilities: imagine how a business might evolve by building a plant in a climate very inhospitable to humans and managing that environment remotely with robotics, once the robots have been properly trained to execute most of the tasks by themselves.

THE ROAD TO SUCCESS IS ALWAYS UNDER CONSTRUCTION. - ARNOLD PALMER (AND ALSO LILY TOMLIN)

As you start mastering the notions of this book, you will acquire an ability to think about each question in multiple layers, especially in the 4th dimension (time). To give an example, your innovation idea may require a complex assembly process that makes it impractical for automation today but if you consider your innovation's timeline planned for launch in twenty-four months, the automation capabilities may be quite advanced by then. Thus, I recommend that you park these questions without a current answer into process blocks that will need to be revisited closer to release date, with a tagged level of uncertainty to weigh the risk associated with this particular innovation.

Reinventing transportation, Sci-Fi style

You have heard it before; 3D printing is a game changer. In fact, all forms of computer remote construction or manipulation is definitely affecting all industries at every level: 3D static and 4D morphing objects printing (4D Printing, s.d.), computer numeric control (CNC) fabrication (CNC, s.d.) and remote-presence manipulation. These modern capabilities have opened the way to implement remote assembly or short-run and custom manufacturing as viable economic alternatives to the standard large-scale fabrication. Short runs especially drive projects to rethink the geographical planning of delivery as robotics costs are comparable across the globe.

In fact, we are getting closer than ever to what we could call teleporting, a form of sending information instead of materials and components to have them build on location, instead of transporting everything all the time with the associated costs in infrastructure, energy and environmental impact. An excellent example of this is with the International Space Station (ISS) where anything you send into orbit, even if it's only a few grams, costs a fortune in cargo fees. The problem is that you cannot work with the principle of "let's send everything just in case" because every item adds to the costs. Instead, NASA is experimenting with 3D printing to simply send raw material; information is then transmitted to print the tools required for the job AS NEEDED ON LOCATION. This is not teleportation but associated with its sibling, 3D scanning, it basically achieves most of its capabilities.

WHAT MAKES THE DESERT BEAUTIFUL IS THAT SOMEWHERE IT HIDES A WELL. - ANTOINE DE SAINT-EXUPERY

AmuseD by Innovation

Chapter Summary
It's essential to identify where you need to focus your attention. Will you rely on the global network to transport goods or to transmit data to build it locally? Will you investigate if certain environments could offer benefits that traditional infrastructure locations do not, such as costs reductions or energy efficiency? As this chapter's name says, it's all about location, location, location. Today's technologies can easily transcend many limitations when it comes to resources, methodologies and locations of activities. In this case, to be frugal can contribute tremendously to the creative process – think that your competition will not shy to use simpler capabilities – with the risk of undercutting your innovation plan.

SPACE IS AN INSPIRATIONAL CONCEPT THAT ALLOWS YOU TO DREAM BIG. - PETER DIAMANDIS

Chapter 10 – Are we there yet?

Topics covered

This chapter is dedicated to one of the most difficult elements to manage on an innovation journey, the timeline. The road to crafting innovation is covered with casualties of war, often because they are either too early for their customers, too late compared to their competitors or the worst-case scenario, just-in-time but not ready – which can happen when a strategic partner does not deliver on its promise. We will study the innovation roadmap and how we can recover from these issues with a good plan.

A bit of history

I started my adult life with a desire to build my career in the life sciences. I loved biology and was fascinated with the countless things misunderstood in this field, particularly in terms of ecosystems and living beings that we could tap and learn from. Microbiology was particularly of interest to me because this was a discipline that involved microbes I could bend to my will within my lifetime. Computers were already very appealing, but I was turned off by coding and did not see myself as a programmer. Besides, the way nature programs randomly and selects optimal features through natural selection was mesmerizing.

Nature is constantly prototyping and discarding what does not work, leaving a constant flow on improvement. Bacteria introduce mutations at the rate of about 5% per generation every 20 minutes: this had the potential to create an entire new set of capabilities within days instead of the normal evolution span of thousands of years for complex species. Viruses provides the means to code with simple nucleic acid triplets using a very economical alphabet (4-5 letters), a deceptively simple mechanism that supplies an entire spectrum of proteins. Sometimes, nature manages to achieve feats that are almost mind-boggling such as overlapping two genes with the same strand of RNA as is the case with the MS2 virus (MS2, s.d.), simply regrouping triplets phased out – starting the reading of the sequence by grouping the same sequence in different triplets. If this can happen with a four genes virus, imagine the challenge of data management for complex species such as humans with about 25 000 genes.

Soon, I realized that managing such a huge amount of information would require the use of computer power. My computer skills were pretty good for the period, and I was eager to put them to good use. Unfortunately, I had pre-empted the introduction of computers in biology as it took almost another ten years to make its way into mainstream research. In a way, you may say that I anticipated the coming of Big data and was ready for it, I just happened to be too soon!

Which is why I am dedicating an entire chapter to this topic. We are going to look at when you should get involved with innovation and when it should be introduced into your product or service lifecycle.

The times, they are a-changin'

The ever so difficult question of "when" is one of the most puzzling one in an innovation agenda. Some may say that you should introduce innovation piecemeal, one feature set at a time, just to keep ahead of your competition. Others will "bundle" innovations and release them as soon as a product or service shows decline. Both strategies are sound, but I will add that both also assume that timing is all up to you. It's not. As mentioned earlier, we are dealing with many internal and external factors. While you may be able to exert force on the internal conditions, there is not much you can do about external ones. These external conditions for which you are reactive can be your customer's shift in interest, the industry's transformation, other competitors' innovations, economic downturn, breakthrough in technology, etc. You get the picture.

There is no silver bullet for this monster. Awareness, iterating regularly and alternative options are the only viable strategies. This is a castle siege where all the food and water in the world will not save you if you are surrounded by the enemy; you need an escape plan. To do this, you need a clear picture of the state of your castle defenses (your innovation capabilities today), your attack strategy (your innovation agenda) and a few escape routes (your roadmap alternatives). If the enemy makes an unexpected move, you can react accordingly.

A timeline of your innovation agenda is immensely useful for this purpose. As you develop your vision for the future of your product or service, you need to start thinking about a broader picture: its iterations in the coming months or years. While I would recommend avoiding looking too far into the future, it is important to define generations of concepts along a timeline. The importance of this is twofold. First, it allows you to either scale down your model or accelerate it depending on external or internal conditions, so Gen-1 and Gen+1 give you leeway without the need to rethink everything. Second, it provides a logical path to other strategic plans that you might have designed, possibly a bridge to a "transnovation" opportunity – nothing says "I have no vision" like a product line that is full of discontinuity or a constant change of target state.

Hurry up, we're waiting

Until the time when we all embrace the singularity (Singularity, s.d.), people may be the most stubborn inhibitor of innovation. Remember that not everyone can absorb change at the same speed; you may have a grandmother that plays videogames online, but I know a lot who are helpless when the car's computer starts asking questions. People cannot be upgraded like machines, and this implies that you need to factor in the speed of people to adapt. Innovation agendas, like any major project that involves people at its core, should not underestimate change management. The best approach to manage this is to treat people in a statistical matter, using a sample population to validate your hypotheses. Any statistics expert will tell you that the key is to use a random subset of individuals to make it the most representative of the population; gaps will soon appear in your innovation agenda that will give you the ability to react in time.

An interesting development is that newer generations are born with change as part of their DNA and in fact often lead it as can be seen with the social media revolution. The difficulty to adapt to change may become less of an issue in the future.

Will we ever bridge the generation gap? I sincerely doubt it; it may even become harder as people live longer, more productive lives. More generations are bound to be working together. Each generation is born and brought up in a social matrix that "gels" in their development years, making any adaptation of communication and collaboration a challenge later in life. Think of it like learning to communicate with a different language; it is always possible to become fluent with an additional language, but it is much easier to master it at a younger age. To prove it, I only need to mention how I struggle to deal with three chat windows on my computer because of the challenge to create compartments in my mind while my kids can manage six different conversations on a cell phone without losing a beat. There might be specific fundamental skills that you need to acquire at a very young age, for which there is no easy remediation. Generation bridging for communication and collaboration is just another innovation opportunity born from social transformations.

Reading in the tea leaves

Sometimes, the best laid plans fall apart because of one crucial part which cannot make it to the party. Nobody has a crystal ball to predict the future; this leaves everyone exposed to the risk that a two-year innovation project may depend on the availability of a key component. If this is on a partner product roadmap, you may be at risk if it is not delivered as expected.

Your other option is to develop your innovation without it but then, how innovative will it be without this key artefact? The recommended approach here is to follow these three principles:

1) Your innovation **should not rely on somebody else's innovation**; it should stand on its own meaning that swapping options will not reduce the value of the entire innovative offering.

EVEN IF YOU'RE ON THE RIGHT TRACK, YOU'LL GET RUN OVER IF YOU JUST SIT THERE. - WILL ROGERS

2) Your innovation **should have more than one key feature** and preferably a lot more; by having many interesting value propositions, your overall risk is reduced if you lose a few.
3) You should always be **able to take an alternate path** or component to make up for the fact that the affected innovative feature cannot be implemented as previously planned.

Examples of this abound. When a new microprocessor is available for computers OEMs, we often witness that many new computers' innovations rely on this single feature. Not only do all the manufacturers' product offerings look the same with similar features but if the microprocessor misses its launch date, all these computer models are released with old components and lose all their appeal...

Chapter Summary

"*May you live in interesting times*" or so the alleged Chinese proverb goes. Change will keep on occurring and proper reaction will be needed; the main difference being how much prepared you are to manage the disruptive event. You cannot stop a fire with the same efficiency using a cup of water or a fire extinguisher. More than anything else, you need to stay on the ball with all the changes that occur around you, whether they are internal or external. Finally, you need to facilitate the change by preparing the transformation of the people affected by the change: they need to be educated, to understand and to embrace the change. The milestones of your innovation path should be journeys with crossroads and alternate routes, with every road leading to your destination.

AmuseD by Innovation

Chapter 11 – Going off-road

Topics covered

In this chapter, we are finally attacking the heart of the subject, what you have all been waiting for: inspiration! This is unfamiliar territory. Buckle your safety belts, keep your hands inside the ride at all times. This is the moment when the magic happens: we explore all the new and exciting capabilities that can help you to introduce new amazing features into your products and services and energize your business.

A bit of history (sort of)

Since this chapter is all about introducing new ways of doing things, I will also introduce this chapter in a different way. Instead of talking about past experiences, I will let your imagination soar. Pretend that we have at our disposal a stylish sports car, pimped up with a time-drive that we rev up until it hits 142 kph launch speed (88 mph for our non-metric friends). Looks like we are heading for the future, thirty years from now, to explore how something as common as fast food is delivered.

First off, we arrive in 2050 on an aerial highway (get it? High-way...) used for GPS-tracked flight-enabled vehicles, as most standard roads are now dedicated either for rented on-demand autonomous vehicles or small one-person mobility units. All these pooled resources are offered to the public for a reasonable fee, which is much more affordable than buying your own vehicle and still provides privacy and personal space. We are visiting our future self who momentarily lives in the suburb of the city; you can relocate any time you want with most of your occasional physical possessions following you, staying at the most convenient shared home unit for your immediate need. In this era, most families do not own homes anymore and communities are still very cohesive, with schools and friends meeting in cyberspace anytime they want.

As you arrive, you are greeted by one of the home robots who leads you to your older self, soaking in a Jacuzzi. As guests have arrived, your future-self calls on a hologram-based service for on-demand lunch ordering. The system

---

THE WRIGHT BROTHERS FLEW RIGHT THROUGH THE SMOKE SCREEN OF IMPOSSIBILITY. - CHARLES F. KETTERING

AmuseD by Innovation

recalls your preferred choices, using a smart mobile computer that is always connected to the home central main hub. Your future-you remain in the pool while running work-related computations and collaborates in real-time with people across the world in their native language. Future-you simply step out of the virtual meeting for a moment to place the order, by talking to a virtual bot who of course recognizes you and presents menu options to your avatar. This is fast-food a la 2050.

The sandwich is created on-demand and the pseudo-meat printed from bio-engineered meat fiber obtained without killing any animals in the process, providing a balanced nutrition for a healthier diet. Bio-engineered meat is made of proteins from microbial culture, much like yogurt, that is not only sustainable but less harmful for the environment as it contributes to reduce the carbon footprint; it requires fewer natural resources and processing than traditional bovine breeding. Newly created menu combinations that were just shared today by worldwide users with the same tastes are also recommended to you to let you try new variations. Payment is easily achieved because of the use of your bio-signature attached to your single-use identity avatar. You could have only purchased the recipe, and have it generated in your home, but the fast-food place has better food printers.

After only a few minutes, the food is ready and sent using common drone-dedicated trains and corridors with machines flying to locations for home delivery at the last mile. The drone delivers the delicious and nutritious food to the home robot, who brings it to you and your guests in person at the pool.

Science-fiction? Probably. Thirty years is a long time, and this may be completely off. In fact, only one prediction about the future is always accurate: you are bound to be wrong at least 50% of the time (if you flip a coin). Yet this is a believable simulation of what might be the life of the future (well, the Jacuzzi might not be but one can wish).

AmuseD by Innovation

All of these innovations can be explored in the following pages using the card format built into the book. I urge you to use them during your brainstorming sessions, they are an effective tool for idea generation.

How to use the cards

Each card is developed as a one-page sheet (let's call it a baseball card) that can be used in workshops and brainstorming sessions. The card, like a sports card analogy, presents a set of attributes that are relevant to the inspiration process of innovation: it presents goals that you might want to address (the "why"), the possible solution component that could address this need (the "how") and the possible use cases that could serve as the base for your innovation project (the "what"). The card analogy is complete with a few examples of known innovations that implement these principles.

It is absolutely necessary to emphasize that you are NOT innovating using these cards, you are creating inspiration through ideas that will enrich your innovation discussions. These random drops of conversations material will foster creativity dialogs, much like a mix and match of random words can create very interesting patterns of poetry (Dada, s.d.). This is why I am not, on purpose, presenting all possible use cases in these cards. First, it would be impossible to imagine all use cases (but you are welcome to try) but furthermore, I want to encourage you to use this to feed your very own expertise and value proposition: your mantra. The result, iterated many times with the input of several people to let it mature like fine wine, will then be ready to be used as the foundation of your innovation agenda.

While you can read each card and start igniting ideas, even fostering interest for more research into each category, it is possible and even recommended to use them within an innovation inspiration workshop. For suggestions on how to proceed at delivering your own workshops, I invite you to look at chapter 16 (the last chapter – you did not really think I would let you get out of reading the entire book, did you?)

IN ORDER TO ATTAIN THE IMPOSSIBLE, ONE MUST ATTEMPT THE ABSURD. - MIGUEL DE CERVANTES

Two innovation methodologies

There are probably as many ways of breaking down innovation ideas as there are stars in the sky. The issue that creeps up when you classify methods is that creating groupings is subject to interpretation; no single classification can handle every case. Even more problematic is the fact that the specific action of breaking them down into groups can introduce more complexity in a model that was built for simplicity.

I have defined a basic classification scheme that I believe can support the most common scenarios. It mirrors two forms of offerings: the product and the service. Based on this premise, the product requires basic resources which are the building material and the actual work of transforming the raw material into a product. The service, on the other hand, defines the result as the end product and the delivery effort as the transformation process. In that sense, we can structure a framework based on two classification schemes: the resource or capacity optimization or the orchestration and/or management optimization.

There is a blurring of the line, as evidenced by the interface of the two spaces in the diagram: in some cases, the fundamental raw material is actually human sourcing. For instance, improvement of ways to execute a job, an orchestration/management optimization scheme, can reduce resources use in terms of energy consumption. Using smart materials in the implementation of a product or service can also ultimately affect and reduce human effort, a resource/capacity optimization.

Using this system, you could create a table where you position resource/capacity optimization on the vertical side and optimization of orchestration/management on the top side, to locate opportunities of innovation at the crossing of these instances.

The following diagram presents this framework.

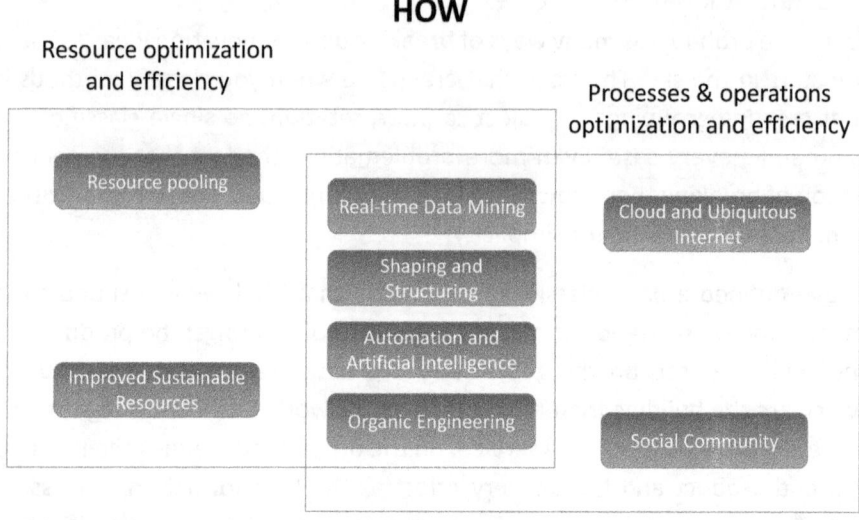

Resource optimization and efficiency

This first methodology is identified as a group of innovation ideas that aim to optimize the resource or capacity of an organization in order to generate modern products and services. Our focus is simple: to do more with less. This is an equation in the sense that you can achieve this through three strategies: increase production, reduce effort or both. The following subsections present all the categories and families in this methodology grouping.

Resource pooling

Category:	RESOURCE POOLING
Family:	Pooling Economics

WHY: Needs addressed / Objectives

- Reduce initial costs of resources infrastructures
- Improve efficiency of resources, ROI
- Distribute or delegate resource management
- Limit liability/ownership of resources or responsibilities
- Streamline resource onboarding
- Provide local assets located where customers need them (convenience)
- Increase ecological and/or sustainable resources

HOW: Attributes and characteristics

- Rent and/or use on-demand easily accessible resources
- Software management for intelligent tracking and resource allocation, often cloud-based for scaling capability
- Service provider acts as a bank for lenders & borrowers with administration fees
- Payment channel
- Membership is open, requiring minimal commitment
- Trust based on reputation of agents, limited liability of agency

WHAT: Possible use cases (incomplete listing)

- Any product use that is attractive but with high ownership cost
- Any product or service with low ROI when dedicated to one customer only
- Low use or yield service to increase its exploitation
- Any product or service with low ROI caused by high shipping or travel costs
- Management of resources exchange or lending for brokerage fees

Examples

- Lyft, UBER, Airbnb --all about resource pooling (also referred as sharing)
- Banking, Savings & Loans and other broker businesses

YOU ARE NEVER TOO OLD TO SET ANOTHER GOAL OR TO DREAM A NEW DREAM. - LES BROWN

AmuseD by Innovation

Category:	RESOURCE POOLING
Family:	Utility-Like Consumption and Transformation

WHY: Needs addressed / Objectives

- Reduce initial costs of resources infrastructures
- Improve efficiency of resources, ROI
- Improve customer affinity and stickiness
- Limit liability/ownership of resources or responsibilities
- Streamline resource onboarding
- Provide simplified resource distribution and usage billing (convenience)
- Increase ecological and/or sustainable resources
- Reduce costly large scale low-value activities

HOW: Attributes and characteristics

- Rent and/or use on-demand easily accessible resources
- Software management for intelligent tracking and resource allocation/consumption metrics/billing, often cloud-based for scaling capability
- Distribution of wholesale bought resources as VAR down-level services
- Payment channel
- Customer onboarding and offloading is automated
- High-value service ensures long term commitment and low customer churning
- Highly mature service model compared to street-level service

WHAT: Possible use cases (incomplete listing)

- Any service use that is attractive but with high ownership or development cost
- Any product or service with low ROI only if dedicated to a single customer
- Low use or yield service to increase resource use through colocation
- Optimized management and cost control of resources fees

Examples

- Cloud and virtualization for maximum elasticity/scalability (including Docker and other software containers technologies)
- Internet APIs for rental pay-per-use software data processing

---

COURAGE IS VERY IMPORTANT. LIKE A MUSCLE, IT IS STRENGTHENED BY USE. - RUTH GORDON

Real-time data mining

Category:	REAL-TIME DATA MINING
Family:	Customer Sentiment Probing

WHY: Needs addressed / Objectives

- Provide better insight into customer interests trends
- Get faster feedback, reviews from potential customers
- Optimize investments plans for new products, services
- Manage risks for innovation projects

HOW: Attributes and characteristics

- Omni channel social networking capabilities to facilitate real-time or near real-time customer opinions
- Cloud-enabled mobile-enabled services for maximum reach, especially in moments of actual product/service consumption (feedback management)
- User experience evaluation framework with next best action tactical response
- User financial commitment capabilities for investments support
- Data warehouse and search engines for managing projects and priorities

WHAT: Possible use cases (incomplete listing)

- New products/service lines testing grounds social network
- Demographics-based and market segments investments planning
- Targeted selling in physical locations or web sites
- Customer management and support services

Examples

- Kickstarter, Indiegogo community product launch pads, supporting community-backed investments interests for projects through a funding baseline
- Amazon web site suggestions for what other similar customers are also buying
- Microsoft Delve to surface common information interests in office groups

AmuseD by Innovation

Category:	REAL-TIME DATA MINING
Family:	Knowledge and Experience Optimization

WHY: Needs addressed / Objectives

- Optimize use of information streaming/ingestion
- Keep up with accelerated skills transformations
- Reduce effort to search for key information
- Surface important information from a large data set
- Extract actionable information from real-time data feeds

HOW: Attributes and characteristics

- Knowledge and skills management system for a classified indexed knowledgebase
- Better search engines algorithms and implementations
- AI assistants
- Skills LMS for efficient career reassignment training (short college periods, constantly in flux, continuous education)
- Real-time data mining
- Information processing hubs, flexible adaptable decision trees
- "Like" tagging and other social networks metadata collections
- AI-suggested docs based on patterns

WHAT: Possible use cases (incomplete listing)

- Intelligent assistants, bots
- Knowledge and skills social networking, social learning (modern LMS)
- Real-time analytics, cognitive algorithms for machine training
- Framework for weighing information relevance, usage
- Visual training aids with mobility support

Examples

- Siri, Cortana, Hey Google personalized interactions
- Google, Bing search engines with prioritized preferred answers
- Facebook and other social networks "like" button to surface people-valued information
- Microsoft Delve and Amazon suggestions for similar interests' reviews
- Real-time event processing engines, AI Machine Learning and patterns training

BE FAITHFUL TO THAT WHICH EXISTS WITHIN YOURSELF. - ANDRE GIDE

AmuseD by Innovation

Shaping and structuring

Category:	SHAPING AND STRUCTURING
Family:	Meta-materials and Composites

WHY: Needs addressed / Objectives

- Reduce weight of product without compromising strength
- Optimize energy use from transporting product for cost savings, sustainability
- Reduce volume of product to free space for new capabilities
- Reduce steps of manufacturing products
- Increase resistance/tolerance to wear and tear
- Introduce innovative design and organic styles, properties, features
- Replace traditional materials with eco-friendly alternatives
- Embed capabilities in non-traditional areas

HOW: Attributes and characteristics

- Physical and chemical properties defined by mesh or 3-dimensional positioning
- Organic inspired technology and architecture

WHAT: Possible use cases (incomplete listing)

- Structural frames in mesh for strength (force distribution) with low weight
- Nano-scale bonding (battery efficiency, molecular-level strength)
- 3D/4D-printed components (including material that changes with stimulus in time), unconventional material products (wood, cement, metal, natural fiber)
- Embedded Electronic circuits or materials for nano-scale space savings
- High-density high-efficiency 3-dimensional architecture

Examples

- Voltera circuit printing printer, 3D printing with many materials at the same time
- New carbon compounds/composites (carbon nanotubes, carbon fiber, q-carbon)
- EXO prosthetic leg for Mesh titanium design, weight reduction
- Airbus Light Rider exoskeleton motorcycle
- Intel XPoint (pronounced Cross-point)
- Non-stick coating for innovative fluid dynamics, Corning Gorilla Glass, BMG elastic glass
- KTH Transparent wood, MesoGlue metal glue, ConFlexPave elastic concrete

---

IMAGINING IS LIKE DREAMING WITH A COMPASS AND A NOTEBOOK. - ME

AmuseD by Innovation

Automation and Artificial Intelligence

Category:	AUTOMATION AND ARTIFICIAL INTELLIGENCE
Family:	On-Demand Construction and Assembly

WHY: Needs addressed / Objectives

- Optimize use of natural resources
- Increase variability and customer personalized/custom assets
- Increase yields and ROI through reduction of waste, unsold products
- Reduce space for product storage waiting to ship
- Reduce human effort (human resources)
- Increase production speed and reduce non-productive time (human resources)

HOW: Attributes and characteristics

- Real-time feedback of customer demand for exact production runs with low inventory requirements
- Profitable customer channel for short-run manufacturing and customization requests (exclusivity factor)
- B2B real-time communication between resource provider, transformation engine and distribution channel
- Small manufacturing facilities with transport automation
- Use of robots, drones
- Use of cloud services infrastructure for scaling on-demand customer requests
- Internet-of-Things (IoT) instrumentation for real-time tracking and monitoring
- AI Human training features for human-task replication

WHAT: Possible use cases (incomplete listing)

- Short-run manufacturing for maximum customer input and choice
- 24/7 plants
- Augmented workforce (automation, robotics and software optimization)

Examples

- Shapeways.com, Domino's pizza delivery by drones, Amazon warehouse robots
- Xbox custom controllers, Adidas Futurecraft 3D printed shoes
- Stratasys multicolor multiple materials including composites 3D printer, Voltera V-One circuit board printer, NVBots for metal 3D printing

---

WHO SEEKS SHALL FIND. - SOPHOCLES

AmuseD by Innovation

Category:	AUTOMATION AND ARTIFICIAL INTELLIGENCE
Family:	High-scale Computing and Artificial Intelligence

WHY: Needs addressed / Objectives

- Highly variable on-demand need for massive computing power (research, etc.)
- Provide near unbreakable cyphers
- Assist human logic with high-speed deterministic automated capability (decision making and non-linear logic)
- Human-like pattern detection at computer speeds
- Huge data sets processing
- Real-time information/attribute detection or recognition

HOW: Attributes and characteristics

- Advanced artificial intelligence modern algorithms
- Cloud-based on-demand scaling for massively parallel processing
- Modern AI-defined computer language and programming to assist in assembling new data models and their exchange of information
- Sophisticated data structures & networking paradigms for highly efficient data cataloging
- Management of apps and processing as a swarm of instances with guaranteed entry, processing and exit point

WHAT: Possible use cases (incomplete listing)

- Cloud providers massive scaling of computational power on demand (clusters)
- Computation capabilities that require heavy initial investments or irregular use that have poor ROI if purchased permanently
- Neural networks or quantum computing
- Fast or real-time processing of complex and/or massive amounts of data to reduce or simplify information retrieval (using reports, dashboards)
- Cognitive pattern recognition, machine learned or human trained

Examples

- Cortana Cognitive services and Azure ML, Google Street View, Google autonomous car
- Data-lake data farming and BI dashboards

MY POWERS ARE ORDINARY. ONLY MY APPLICATION BRINGS ME SUCCESS. - ISAAC NEWTON

AmuseD by Innovation

Organic engineering

Category:	ORGANIC ENGINEERING
Family:	Inspired/Leveraged Biological Manufacturing

WHY: Needs addressed / Objectives

- Increase efficiency of production yields
- Provide more ecologically minded, sustainable product alternatives
- Improve efficiency of products and materials
- Access product features that are difficult or not economically profitable to reproduce using traditional techniques

HOW: Attributes and characteristics

- Protein, cellular or nucleic acid-based technology for increased performance and/or more limited areas of targeted action
- Often "grown or bred" components with additional chemical refinement steps

WHAT: Possible use cases (incomplete listing)

- Protein-based fibers or resins that are stronger than their artificial counterparts
- Ribonucleic acids as data storage and exchange for redundancy, resiliency and data density
- Highly specialized proteins for unique features, capabilities
- Animals, insects or microbes genetically engineered to produce highly efficient silk protein for weaving modern textiles
- Nano-bots' components grown from substrate templates
- Concentrating low yield products into more efficient harvesting methods
- Bio-degradable containers made from natural waxes and plants fiber
- Molecular biochemistry multi-steps transformation through the use of environment-controlled microbial vats for efficient processing of material

Examples

- Woven bamboo-based fiber and resin products as alternative for artificial fiber
- Spider silk as alternative produced by genetically engineered goats in their milk to develop fiber-like textiles for an advantageous strength-to-weight ratio
- DNA-based data storage for remarkable information storage density and resiliency
- Rhodopsin-based light activated medium for computer storage

---

SUCCESS IS FINDING SATISFACTION IN GIVING A LITTLE MORE THAN YOU TAKE. - CHRISTOPHER REEVE

Improved sustainable resources

Category:	IMPROVED SUSTAINABLE RESOURCES
Family:	Renewable/Recoverable Energy Resources

WHY: Needs addressed / Objectives

- Increase energy density per weight
- Reduce dependency on rare or expensive non-sustainable materials
- Reduce carbon footprint or negative ecological impact
- Increase efficiency or provide energy independence through self-sustenance

HOW: Attributes and characteristics

- Utilization of the capabilities of the local environment to provide parts of the energy generating equation
- Avoids non-sustainable limited access materials (such as rare-earth metals that are expensive and hard to mine at high yield)
- Simplified infrastructure required to transport the energy where it is needed – consumption is usually very closely located to energy capture
- Recycling of systems by-products to assist in electric power generation (mechanical, heat transfer, solar, wind, water, etc.)
- Sustainable, recyclable and ecological

WHAT: Possible use cases (incomplete listing)

- Self-sustaining machines and/or instruments that do not need energy distribution infrastructure
- Longer lasting lighter electronic components for energy storage
- Areas with poor infrastructure development to provide local energy access

Examples

- Bio-batteries made from either microbes or microbial generated products for high-density molecular dynamos, carbon-14 nuclear waste crushed into diamonds recycled as thousand years long lasting batteries
- Bio-inspired chloroplasts-like solar energy generators using none of the dangerous or limited access metals like Selenium, Germanium, Gallium or Cadmium, surface plasmon resonances
- Roads that capture the energy created by the weight displacement of cars with pressure plates into batteries to turn on streetlights; clothes that capture energy from motion

---

I HAVE ALWAYS BEEN MORE INTERESTED IN EXPERIMENT, THAN IN ACCOMPLISHMENT. - ORSON WELLES

AmuseD by Innovation

Category:	IMPROVED SUSTAINABLE RESOURCES
Family:	Earth citizenship

WHY: Needs addressed / Objectives

- Reduce carbon-footprint and greenhouse gas emissions
- Reduce overall negative impact to the environment and biosphere
- Improve use of carbon-neutral materials and resources
- Address needs caused by population growth and change in demographics
- Address social transformations caused by urbanisation on a global scale

HOW: Attributes and characteristics

- Optimized transportation schemes, fuel use and roads
- Use of digital convergence, robotics and avatars to support tele-working
- Use of biologically made materials to reduce carbon-footprint
- Use of remote instrumentation and Internet-of-things (IoT) to collect measurements without moving
- Electronic or software manipulation and upgrades
- Optimized human required resources (food, utilities, energy)

WHAT: Possible use cases (incomplete listing)

- Remote presence devices
- Drones and robots to reduce human transportation
- Road optional product delivery (flying and swimming drones, electronic data delivery, 3D printing for remote product shipping)
- Last mile environment-friendly mobility devices
- AR/VR simulated collaboration and communication environments

Examples

- Electric scooters or rent-stations for last mile transportation from a community service
- Remotely operated robot surgeon without specialist displacement
- Software upgrades & call-home for modern Internet-connected intelligent devices
- Domino's drone pizza delivery, Just Eat and Starship Technologies robot delivery service
- Electric solar collection roofs for grid assistance from Tesla

EVERY EXIT IS AN ENTRY SOMEWHERE ELSE. - TOM STOPPARD

AmuseD by Innovation

Category:	IMPROVED SUSTAINABLE RESOURCES
Family:	Geographical Opportunistic Environment Use

WHY: Needs addressed / Objectives

- Reduce costs from climate control premises management
- Change impact of unavoidable climate change effects from negative to positive

HOW: Attributes and characteristics

- Relocation of services in global locations with naturally occurring desirable environment attributes (extreme cold, heat, dry or humid, etc.)
- Minimal infrastructure required to import/export products to the new location with reduced transport requirements
- Devices or components that can exploit side-effects of significant climate change as non-permanent benefits to reduce environment footprint and fight global warming

WHAT: Possible use cases (incomplete listing)

- Use extreme cold areas for natural air conditioning
- Use extremely inhospitable areas that are too hot or toxic for humans to host robot-managed resource processing services that can be routed (solar or wind energy, electronic storage, etc.)

Examples

- Svalbard Global permafrost seeds bank for disaster relief
- Rising tides watermills for clean sustainable localized energy production such as plants from EnergyBC, Sihwa Lake tidal power plant
- Solar farms in growing desert land to generate clean energy
- Facebook's Sweden Datacenter natural cooling in the arctic with network cabling grid

---

WE WILL EITHER FIND A WAY, OR MAKE ONE. - HANNIBAL

AmuseD by Innovation

Processes & operations optimization and efficiency

This second methodology is identified as a group of innovation ideas that aim to optimize the processes and/or operations of an organization in generating modern products and services. The focus of this optimization is to introduce smart communication and collaboration through the pervasive use of ubiquitous commoditized digital technology and modern cloud-powered massive computing capabilities that enable widespread business empowerment. The following subsections present all the categories and families in this methodology grouping.

Automation and Artificial Intelligence

Category:	AUTOMATION AND ARTIFICIAL INTELLIGENCE
Family:	Workforce Synergy and Expansion

WHY: Needs addressed / Objectives

- Optimize workforce made up of many different generations
- Take advantage of handicapped or limited ability individuals in the workforce
- Collaborate better through language, culture and distance barriers

HOW: Attributes and characteristics

- Social tools adaptable to every workstyle
- Augmented workforce (cybernetic worker)
- AR and VR simulation capabilities for immersive location-agnostic collaboration
- Real-time language translation

WHAT: Possible use cases (incomplete listing)

- Robot/drone remote training (task learning) and piloting (gaming experience)
- Cybernetic prosthetics or cyber enhancements (such as wearables, cameras, etc.) for augmented workforce
- Artificial Intelligence (AI) assisted activities for cognitive or physical disabilities
- Real-time language translation communication
- AR or VR environment simulated space for face-to-face collaboration
- Autonomous vehicles with artificial human-inspired vision (liDar, etc.)

Examples

- Drone fleet pilots' headquarters, Fraunhofer IPA/Max Planck Institute suspended VR cabin
- Chat bots such as Slack Bot, Microsoft Bot Framework
- Slack and Microsoft Teams for social interactions adaptable to user needs
- Skype real-time translator with user voice simulation for real-time communication across language barriers
- AI generated machine-generated compositions such as MIT's deep-learning videos
- Skype sessions with Microsoft HoloLens at NASA for mars exploration real-time collaboration and simulation

AmuseD by Innovation

Category:	AUTOMATION AND ARTIFICIAL INTELLIGENCE
Family:	Resource Allocation and Orchestration

WHY: Needs addressed / Objectives

- Optimize and schedule activities heavily influenced by external factors
- Improve efficiency of inter-related tasks and activities that have many dependencies

HOW: Attributes and characteristics

- Cloud-based "smart" solution to track multiple elements and coordinate best outcome in real-time
- "Robo-boss" form of task assignment deployed to users for immediate notification of intervention planning
- Additional data streams of external agents that may impact decision making (weather, traffic, etc.)
- Dynamic resource allocation assisted by bidirectional data feeds (status to action)
- Real-time mobile communication network
- Expert system or knowledge library to support optimal interventions efficiency
- Human physical and behavioral monitoring with emotions detection

WHAT: Possible use cases (incomplete listing)

- Mobile fleet of technicians dispatched along an optimized list of clients' interventions
- AI-based smart processes that recalculate optimized inter-related project steps dynamically as the work progresses or stalls to ensure efficient advancement

Examples

- Uber/Lyft service provider and client matching service for efficient dispatch
- GPS-location assigned truck fleet mappings and routes for package delivery
- SmartDispatching.com

YOU MUST BE THE CHANGE YOU WISH TO SEE IN THE WORLD. - GANDHI

Category:	AUTOMATION AND ARTIFICIAL INTELLIGENCE
Family:	Nano Technology

WHY: Needs addressed / Objectives

- Reduce assets losses
- Optimize energy and resources consumption for surveying

HOW: Attributes and characteristics

- Micrometer-scale mechanics and robotics
- Remotely induced data transmission through modern electronic antennas
- Chemical or electromagnetic power generation to remove the need for local onboard batteries
- Swarm-like and/or mesh dynamic intelligent networking
- Intelligent location-aware mobility tracking

WHAT: Possible use cases (incomplete listing)

- Enclosed environment small scale surveying and monitoring
- Small surgical interventions in very limited access environments
- Smart dust for tracking and identifying shipments and products

Examples

- Micro-drone swarms for low footprint, large areas detailed coverage
- RFID and Active RFID-based micro-tags for non-invasive radio-based container tracking
- RoboFly Lentink-Dickinson model for low-energy microbot flight, DGIST ciliary microrobotics
- UC Boulder pliable multi-purpose 3g acoustic sensor

AmuseD by Innovation

Real-time data mining

Category:	REAL-TIME DATA MINING
Family:	Knowledge and Information Use Optimization

WHY: Needs addressed / Objectives

- Process data faster to get accurate on-demand time-sensitive information
- Identify data that is relevant in a much more efficient manner
- Detect trends in single or multiple inter-related systems

HOW: Attributes and characteristics

- Massive data storage capabilities (data warehouse) and data ingestion flows
- Pre-processing triage capabilities based on rules
- Multi-dimensional views and analytics for maximum correlation visibility
- AI capabilities to apply data cataloging techniques based on human guidance or through machine learning frameworks
- Trend or decision post-processing system to provide next best action
- User feedback capabilities for additional data channel

WHAT: Possible use cases (incomplete listing)

- Real-time faster than human decision making to take next best action based on specific set of circumstances
- Pattern recognition on a massive scale with very large amounts of data and/or channels to correlate
- Knowledge management for surfacing most important, useful information to reduce human learning curve (Expert system)
- Customer feedback, demographics product and/or service alignment

Examples

- Google Face recognition processing for massive image libraries
- Apple Siri or Microsoft Cortana speech recognition and action
- Amazon suggestion for next purchase based on similar customer interests' patterns across many products, demographics, channels
- Indiegogo and Kickstarter customer product interest based on selected funding affinity
- Wayz real-time users' locations analyzed for traffic condition and processed to provide a simple view of the most efficient routes to a destination

GRACE IS THE BEAUTY OF FORM UNDER THE INFLUENCE OF FREEDOM. - FRIEDRICH VON SCHILLER

AmuseD by Innovation

Category:	REAL-TIME DATA MINING
Family:	Machine-to-Machine Communication

WHY: Needs addressed / Objectives

- Efficient intelligent machine and software communication
- High-speed conditional data handshake and processing

HOW: Attributes and characteristics

- Common set of language taxonomy and syntax for machines to connect securely, adapted to one or many levels of machine complexity
- Shareable technology for machines to expose to each other capabilities that can be discovered and utilized
- Trusting framework and entity to provide security, authentication, intimate communication, non-repudiation
- Resilient or tolerant network connection for machine linking
- Channel assignment for one-to-one, one-to-many or many-to-many connections

WHAT: Possible use cases (incomplete listing)

- Machine to machine interactions for quick, efficient always-on analysis at scale
- Autonomous robotics, drones or vehicles' real-time location awareness for collision avoidance and collaboration
- Consumables browsing and purchasing for Intelligent autonomous devices
- Swarm and cluster processing for scale-out data manipulation scenarios

Examples

- Tesla auto-pilot car system and Google autonomous car for vehicle self-driving
- Intelligent network storage drive failure notification to service center
- Printer with defined manufacturer specs and purchase rules connected to a provider network for ordering toner by itself
- Quadcopters working in cooperation to survey a piece of land from the air

---

IT IS NEVER TOO LATE TO BE WHAT YOU MIGHT HAVE BEEN. - GEORGE ELIOT

AmuseD by Innovation

Category:	REAL-TIME DATA MINING
Family:	Machine-to-Human Modern Communication

WHY: Needs addressed / Objectives

- Human health and state awareness and/or monitoring
- Unbiased measurement of human workforce efficiency

HOW: Attributes and characteristics

- Some form of instrument or camera to take time-stamped measurements, located appropriately in a room or as a wearable attached to the user, to allow the most reliable stream of data
- Common set of language taxonomy and syntax for machines to connect securely, adapted to one or many levels of machine complexity
- Common way for machines to expose to each other capabilities that can be discovered and utilized
- Trusting framework and entity to provide security, authentication, intimate communication, non-repudiation
- Resilient or tolerant network connection for machine linking
- Channel assignment for one-to-one, one-to-many or many-to-many connections

WHAT: Possible use cases (incomplete listing)

- Human health monitoring for dangerous or hazardous work that can only be performed by humans
- Workforce location and status view for efficient dispatch of resources
- Biofeedback and/or biometric authentication
- Human emotional measurement for workforce management and optimization

Examples

- Windows Hello facial recognition login and Apple fingerprint iDevice unlocking
- IoT bracelet or smartwatches with health monitoring and alerting for patients at risk of losing consciousness or unaware of health deterioration
- Emotional detection in facial API for depression early warning
- Machine-driven therapy based on real-time physical and emotional stress metrics

---

WHEN ONE MUST, ONE CAN. - CHARLOTTE WHITTON

Shaping and structuring

Category:	SHAPING AND STRUCTURING
Family:	Augmented Reality Workforce Enablement

WHY: Needs addressed / Objectives

- Reduce costs of prototyping
- Reduce costly architectural or engineering mistakes requiring significant remodeling at a late stage
- Optimize knowledge and skills across long distances
- Improve visualization and modifications activities with reduced resources

HOW: Attributes and characteristics

- Virtual/Augmented/Mixed Reality 3D software modeling space to visualize simulations of products
- Powerful graphics systems to model 3D shapes in software in real-time at scale
- Devices to interact in 3D simulated space (including view, motion tracking and manipulation capabilities)
- Communication and/or some form of established contact with the real world
- Networking capabilities with resilient or tolerant network
- Feedback capabilities for two-way sensory input

WHAT: Possible use cases (incomplete listing)

- Remote collaboration in immersive 3D space between distant unrelated parties
- Supplemental data feeds and location of referenced data in real-time
- Models' simulation, engineering and prototyping without consuming physical resources or manufacturing capabilities to the limits of the finished product
- User point-of-view and feedback without manufacturing
- Robot or drone control with accurate transmission of actual environment

Examples

- NASA Mars rover simulation using Microsoft Hololens in collaborative mode
- HTC Vive real-time vehicle model simulation and editing with user feedback
- Augmented data overlay of Google data from Google Maps and GPS
- Robot remote control in surgery room located hundreds of kilometers away

---

OUT OF DIFFICULTIES GROW MIRACLES. - JEAN DE LA BRUYÈRE

AmuseD by Innovation

Category:	SHAPING AND STRUCTURING
Family:	Open-Source Hardware

WHY: Needs addressed / Objectives

- Reduce R&D costs for the discovery and implementation of new technologies
- Concentration of efforts on customer interest and value creation
- Increase synergy of strategic partners
- Improve brand value through industry feedback and participation (influence)
- Increase potential customer and/or business partner feedback
- Improve customer loyalty with products that gain value with time instead of programmed obsolescence

HOW: Attributes and characteristics

- Use of open-source licensing models for legal protection
- Social media or collaboration engine to support active development
- Social community participation or contribution through legal or financial model
- Common or compatible set of simulation and CAD tools
- Documents and procedures repository with versioning and metadata search
- Smart objects that gain new features through remote upgrades

WHAT: Possible use cases (incomplete listing)

- Modular systems with common interfaces for ecosystem development
- Business model for selling products and services enhanced or inspired by the community
- Software-based on-demand functions (micro-services, APIs) and other consumption-based technologies that enrich the global ecosystem
- Products that can download new code from the Internet through subscription
- Morphing objects for maximum adaptability (including architecture, buildings)

Examples

- Keurig beverage cups open cup market for industry participation
- International Space Station (ISS) common interface modules
- Red Hat Linux business model (both community and enterprise level services)
- Microsoft Facial recognition API micro-service for developing rich cloud-based apps with reduced effort and infrastructure resources
- Tesla cars microcode that can be upgraded with new features over time

---

HOW DO YOU KNOW YOU'RE GOING TO DO SOMETHING, UNTIL YOU DO IT? - J. D. SALINGER

AmuseD by Innovation

Category:	SHAPING AND STRUCTURING
Family:	Workforce Enhancements and Optimization

WHY: Needs addressed / Objectives

- Improve human workforce tasks not easily automated or replaced by robots/drones
- Provide sensory or physical capabilities not naturally available in humans
- Reduce the work impact of disabilities
- Reduce the need for highly valuable human or human-sourced limited resources
- Improve effectiveness of work using synergistic features

HOW: Attributes and characteristics

- Use of organic-inspired or compatible highly efficient technologies to enhance natural capabilities to supernatural levels
- 3D materials and metamaterials with unique properties to either mimic or interface with human hosts (at the cellular, limb or organ level)
- Technologies that take advantage of human activity side-effects in naturally occurring activities

WHAT: Possible use cases (incomplete listing)

- Composites and metamaterials that make use of human normal activity (heat, movement, environment transformation) to recover energy, resources
- Custom organic-compatible mesh compound used in 3D printing to build replacement bones matrix, populated and eventually replaced by normal cells
- Enhanced sensory inputs (augmented vision, auditory translation of frequencies, etc.) through wearables for improved efficiency field work
- Exoskeletons for human-like movement with increased strength or speed
- Handicap prosthetics custom-made for specific tools and purposes manufactured per individual in a cost-efficient manner (3D printing)
- Synthesized human artefacts with equivalent or superior efficiency such as human hormones or blood by-products

Examples

- Honda exoskeleton to lift very heavy loads, reduced need to walk and sit
- Embedded battery metamaterial in clothes that recharges with casual movements
- Organic biological replacements (biodegradable mesh) or prosthesis for missing limbs and handicaps

---

THE SECRET OF GETTING AHEAD IS GETTING STARTED. - MARK TWAIN

AmuseD by Innovation

Cloud and ubiquitous Internet

Category:	CLOUD AND UBIQUITOUS INTERNET
Family:	Network and Communication Everywhere

WHY: Needs addressed / Objectives

- Access data, applications, machines and people where they need to be at any time and from anywhere
- Reduce time and effort to initiate on-demand exchange of information
- Simplify and make strategic use of freely available information
- Improve computer processing and costs by displacing complex tasks to more powerful infrastructures as needed

HOW: Attributes and characteristics

- New proximity and line-of-sight networking technology for last-mile networking (LiFi, 5G mesh, AllJoyn IoT, IPv6, new high-density networking such as 2.5G and 5G Ethernet over existing Cat6 cables)
- High-bandwidth network concentrators or hubs to attach less intelligent and more numerous devices to the Internet
- Cloud computing services and artificial intelligence (including neural networks)
- Internet-of-things (IoT) solutions and capabilities for smart device control
- Remote control from a dashboard piloting headquarters for orchestration and management

WHAT: Possible use cases (incomplete listing)

- Remote work or processing displacement
- Connected individual and site (work and home)
- On-demand smart device data interchange with remote onsite orchestration

Examples

- Passive RFID and/or NFC for low-speed proximity simplified data exchange such as key card validation, Active RFID for longer distance more involved data communication such as electronic road toll collection
- Car location sharing awareness from a short distance for autonomous driving
- Security personnel wearable cameras
- Human language recognition by displacing actual speech analysis to the cloud instead of processing it locally on a limited personal device (phone)

CAN YOU IMAGINE WHAT I WOULD DO IF I COULD DO ALL I CAN? - JEFF RICH

AmuseD by Innovation

Category:	CLOUD AND UBIQUITOUS INTERNET
Family:	Identity and Security Protection

WHY: Needs addressed / Objectives

- Protect sensitive data from unauthorized use and secure the communication channel from eavesdropping or altering its content
- Simplify non-repudiation of actions
- Guarantee that origin and destination of communication channel are who they are supposed to be
- Simplify security to achieve a safe and reliable authentication process

HOW: Attributes and characteristics

- Use of software encryption and electronic keys or certificates
- Use of secure communication technology for networks (IPsec, IPv6)
- Trusting framework and entity to provide security, authentication, intimate communication, non-repudiation
- Active defense mechanisms (intrusion prevention, attack push-back and defense, alteration of data stream controls, etc.)
- Time-stamp technology for accurate traceability and correlation of events
- Logging of actions
- Facilities to manage synchronous (database) or asynchronous (queuing, blockchain) data capture to guarantee the quality of the data using non-repudiated actions in a reliable form

WHAT: Possible use cases (incomplete listing)

- Machines transactions and automated payments
- Remote control of dangerous or hazardous equipment
- Secure human biometrics-based access control
- Protection of highly secured data transmission and/or communication
- Traceability and replay control of specific events or sequences of events

Examples

- Robot control for remote surgery in an operating room
- Printer purchasing consumables such as toner directly on the Internet by itself
- IoT wearable data for updating a patient state of health with remote healthcare
- Bitcoin technology as a global distributed currency with decentralized authority

SUCCESS IS THE MAXIMUM UTILIZATION OF THE ABILITY THAT YOU HAVE. - ZIG ZIGLAR

AmuseD by Innovation

Social community

Category:	SOCIAL COMMUNITY
Family:	Open Source Everything

WHY: Needs addressed / Objectives

- Reduce the effort required in testing and iterating on less strategic components and make them more reliable
- Reduce development time by reusing readily accessible material and applying limited modifications or customization
- Increase market footprint by creating or participating in a product ecosystem
- Develop and foster client/partner synergies that can affect product evolution
- Benefit from 3rd-party/external feedback on product/service results & improvement areas
- Reduce negative impact of bugs/issues

HOW: Attributes and characteristics

- Collaboration framework with possible external access
- Social network capabilities
- Use of open-source licensing models for legal protection
- Universal protocols for data exchange (XML and derivatives)
- Documents and procedures repository with versioning and metadata
- Search and classification engines to improve open-source documents tracking
- Self-sufficiency to fix bugs/issues in a timely manner by accessing components sources and recipes (in-house development teams)
- Open publicly accessible ecosystem design documents

WHAT: Possible use cases (incomplete listing)

- Community engineering of social needs; OpenMDAO Hyperloop development model
- Collaboration convergence sites for idea incubation (hackathons, etc.)
- Public Internet feedback sites for product beta testing

Examples

- X-prize to foster competition of ideas
- Open-source operating system such as Linux, Amazon Alexa ecosystem
- Moto smartphone Mods development kit for Moto Z compatible modules

---

ACTION IS ELOQUENCE. - WILLIAM SHAKESPEARE

AmuseD by Innovation

Category:	SOCIAL COMMUNITY
Family:	Diversity Optimized Collaboration

WHY: Needs addressed / Objectives

- Increase customer demographics
- Optimize workforce collaboration around specific skillsets
- Location independent best fit expertise
- Increase product or service marketability to support global aspirations

HOW: Attributes and characteristics

- Tools to override language barriers
- Collaboration framework with possible external access
- Social network capabilities
- Multi-channel communication capabilities with aggregation of connections adaptable to every need, preference, requirement or constraint
- Multi-format document & assets management storage, search capabilities and metadata
- Information surfacing engine for active sharing and suggestions of common interests through diverse channels

WHAT: Possible use cases (incomplete listing)

- Global projects communities
- Local centers of excellence crossing demographics boundaries (country of origin, culture, age, language)
- Social learning engines for optimized knowledge transfer targeted to most effective methods for different groups of individuals
- Real-time language independent project collaboration (active translation)

Examples

- Company-wide global social networks
- Skype real-time translation
- MongoDB content aggregation for documents, YouTube videos
- Microsoft Delve suggestions for common interests, Insiders early adopters' program
- Facebook "like" and Twitter keywords to trigger followed interests

REVOLUTIONS ARE NOT MADE; THEY COME. - WENDELL PHILLIPS

AmuseD by Innovation

Category:	SOCIAL COMMUNITY
Family:	Enhanced Prototyping

WHY: Needs addressed / Objectives

- Iterate and evolve products and services faster
- Discover what is unknown, explore unfamiliar territory
- Embrace new ideas more easily
- Reduce the obstacles of visualizing concepts and sharing them early
- Facilitate access to the manipulation of early prototypes

HOW: Attributes and characteristics

- Immersive software-based realistic simulation, often either AR/VR/MR based
- 3D, CNC or other devices to build quickly concept iterations with a fail-fast approach to exploration
- Physical "primitives" electronics modules to provide early conceptual familiarity to the project team (blocks, connectors, interlocking components)
- Social network capabilities to improve team and/or external feedback
- Collaborative solutions to support dialog
- Document management system with multimedia capabilities and metadata search to support versioning and forking of project development

WHAT: Possible use cases (incomplete listing)

- Innovation lab environment to accelerate and foster the testing of concepts
- Simulated reality space to explore concepts before they are physically built
- Small scale manufacturing facility for concepts
- Incubation groups of non-mainstream products or services exploration

Examples

- Envelop software improved development workflow
- East Carolinian Augmented Reality topography simulation
- 3D printers that can make electronic circuits (Voltera) and even magnets (University Service Centre for Transmission Electron Microscopy in Vienna, Austria)
- CrossBeams and K'Nex toys for quick prototyping, Google Labs, Microsoft Garage

---

BELIEVE YOU CAN AND YOU'RE HALFWAY THERE. - THEODORE ROOSEVELT

AmuseD by Innovation

Category:	SOCIAL COMMUNITY
Family:	Record-based Reputation and Affinity

WHY: Needs addressed / Objectives

- Capture time-sensitive customer satisfaction & sentiment, reduce customer churning
- Establish a more trusting long-term relationship with customers
- Identify and promote most valuable actions or people in an organization
- Provide a platform for effective assets to grow and outperform

HOW: Attributes and characteristics

- Social networking capabilities with freeform interactions and support for "Like" tagging to surface important content, follow key individuals
- Links to strategic projects to capture early feedback
- "Beta" or "insider" seeding programs for customers with stronger risk appetite
- Feedback system with analytics (data mining) to aggregate and share insight
- AI system to analyze surfaced relevant information and suggest it to other people with similar interests, roles
- Rewards based on a meritocracy form of performance review for top-performers and distinguished strategic assets (track records)

WHAT: Possible use cases (incomplete listing)

- Customer digital channel with exclusive rewards, early access "VIP" or white glove programs for early adopters (loyalty programs)
- Corporate internal system to track documents, comments, suggestions and other shared insight that can be evaluated by peers for usefulness and promoted to the top of search lists, suggested topics
- Project steering committees with social network links for maximum transparency/integration of continuous improvement dialogs

Examples

- Amazon's suggestions to sell what others like you are buying, Microsoft Office Delve for suggested documents interests of similar roles
- Rewards and loyalty programs
- Uber, Lyft, Airbnb members "reputations" to provide confidence to customers

---

WONDER RATHER THAN DOUBT IS THE ROOT OF ALL KNOWLEDGE. - ABRAHAM JOSHUA HESCHEL

AmuseD by Innovation

Category:	SOCIAL COMMUNITY
Family:	Modular Architecture

WHY: Needs addressed / Objectives

- Provide a platform for effective assets to grow and outperform
- Establish long term relationships with customers and partners
- Simplify and enrich customer experience
- Provide better customized solutions to grow customer base

HOW: Attributes and characteristics

- Software integration points that facilitate interoperability
- Discrete components with clearly purposed and delimited set of features and/or characteristics
- Components that can exchange information using standardized methods
- Collaboration framework with possible external access
- Universal protocols for data exchange (XML and derivatives)
- Documents and procedures repository with versioning and metadata
- Open publicly accessible collaboration ecosystem to design documents

WHAT: Possible use cases (incomplete listing)

- Offer software or cloud-based services that can be consumed on demand and billed for service use as part of customers' applications
- Offer a service to customers that simplifies product or service consumption to become an integral part of the offering matrix model
- Product offered in a general format that can be easily customized or adapted for niche scenarios to foster an ecosystem of partners with their own innovations and grow the customer base by adding fringe use cases

Examples

- Apple, Google Android and Windows universal apps App stores ecosystems
- Microsoft Azure Cognitive APIs micro-services and Azure Functions
- Apple iPhone and iPad ecosystem with compatible connector product lines
- Moto Z smartphones with modular pluggable components

IT ALWAYS SEEMS IMPOSSIBLE UNTIL IT'S DONE. - NELSON MANDELA

Organic engineering

Category:	ORGANIC ENGINEERING
Family:	Biology-Inspired Enhancements

WHY: Needs addressed / Objectives

- Improve the reliability and effectiveness of operations
- Increase reach of operations
- Reduce human risk
- Improve ecological and sustainable practices
- Reduce costs of operations, optimize time of data gathering

HOW: Attributes and characteristics

- Use of biological compounds or nature-inspired techniques or materials
- Laboratory capabilities to harness and maintain biology-inspired compounds
- Farming model to sustain biological workforce
- Cloud or cluster-based high-speed volume calculations to manage swarms of IoT or robot/drone capable technologies (including piloted organisms)
- Dashboard command center to manage assets
- Communication resilient or tolerant network for remote control of assets

WHAT: Possible use cases (incomplete listing)

- Mimic insect attributes in small drones to cover large areas or inhospitable terrain in the form of remote-controlled swarms
- Bird flock inspired flight patterns in drones to avoid mid-air collisions
- Self-regulating systems that mimic the principles of animal population control in nature, reducing the individuals when food becomes scarce
- Attach tools and/or robots to living creatures to capture sensory information (camera) and pilot them to reach areas not easily manageable by robots

Examples

- Controls for flying drones/animals to simplify decision-making process, inspect areas, mapping of terrain, map disaster area for survivors
- Autonomous cars swarm-like location exchange for environment awareness

SUCCESS CONSISTS OF GOING FROM FAILURE TO FAILURE WITHOUT LOSS OF ENTHUSIASM. - WINSTON CHURCHILL

AmuseD by Innovation

Chapter Summary

This chapter covered a lot of ground to link the "why", the "what" and the "how". Already, you should have reached one of two states at this moment:

1. You are intrigued by these innovation ideas concepts, and you want to learn more about them.
2. You are inspired by these innovation ideas concepts and would like to see how they can be combined, together or with your own uniqueness.

Congratulations, you have graduated to the point where you have a solid grasp of the many modern trends available today and are excited about exploring their numerous benefits for your business needs. Inspiration is the key to innovation.

Next, we will work at answering the remaining questions to finalize the foundation of your innovation agenda.

Chapter 12 – Who, tell me who

Topics covered

This chapter is devoted to the question of "who". This might seem obvious in terms of who your innovation is planned for, with details likely to be handled by your market research. You may be surprised to know however that the next wave of digital customers will not be swayed in the same fashion as they used to be. Just like you want to learn more about your customers, they also learn more about you and give you the appropriate feedback; knowledge and opinion are becoming very valuable. It is as the great Yogi Berra once said: *"half the lies they tell about me aren't true"*. Finally, we will review the repercussions of customer sentiment as we mitigate negative opinions and take advantage of positive feedback. Human relations are on the verge of a tectonic shift, let's hope it's not the Big One.

A bit of history

I once met a CxO for a discussion about innovation and one of the topics that surfaced involved automation and robotics. Right away, I knew I had touched a nerve when he immediately told me that this subject was to be avoided from future conversations. He was adamant about the fact that he did not want to talk about robots, automation or artificial intelligence. His reaction was obviously motivated by personal experience since it seemed to carry so much negative emotion. Being an open advocate of automation, I inquired about his experience; I felt it was in my best interest to know all the aspects of this subject, both good and bad.

He was very candid and explained his reason: he was handling large amounts of complaints from customers about their phone menu selection system and how bad the user experience was in handling customers, so much so that most users simply dialed "0" to talk to a person and avoided all the unfriendly menu levels. I could not agree more; I hate those systems myself. We formed a bridge of empathy over a common malaise.

I then noticed that he had an iPhone lying on his desk. I casually asked if he used the Siri feature on his phone by asking questions to the system such as how the weather is or schedule an appointment; I was curious what he thought of this experience. He acknowledged that it was decent, with an interested look in his eye. I suggested to him that Siri is a "bot" just like his bad phone system, albeit a much more sophisticated one that seems to give him a satisfactory – or at least tolerable – user experience.

I shared with him my theory that his objection to robots and automation was not necessarily directed at automation or AI in general but most probably that instead he was frustrated by "dumb" technology. I hinted at the fact that his customers (and him) might feel different if they experienced a "smart" conversation with an automated AI that felt more natural and could relate to a customer's need in one sentence, not a long menu of options. Finally, I mentioned that the intelligence of that kind of "bot" could easily be tapped by his business as it is now readily available…

Needless to say, that robotic conversation took a different turn. This demonstrates that communication is unmistakably a two-way system and that thinking about only one side of the communication, asking for the customer to provide all the intelligence, can degrade and eventually break the user experience rather quickly. In this day and age, as we are now seeing more human-to-machine and machine-to-machine conversations than the human-to-human kind, it is imperative to enable communications that are designed for maximum effectiveness between the two parties.

Hello, is it me you're looking for?

What is truly outstanding in the modern world is that globalization, world communication and pervasive Internet all contribute to increase the rate of change, happening in months instead of decades, which basically changes people very quickly as well. Following demographics and customer sentiment evolution are becoming critical in any business since, just like a plague can now cross continents in hours to become a pandemic, bad publicity can spread like wildfire. This goes beyond knowing your customers to nurture a tight, intimate relationship. You need to develop a rapport where you feel like the confidant, an individual who is deeply aware of this

---

IF YOU DOUBT YOURSELF ALL THE TIME, REMEMBER TO LISTEN TO OTHERS WHEN THEY PRAISE YOU. - ME

bipolar friend you need to keep an eye on. Customer demographics and analytics can help you keep tabs on this mighty morphin' power stranger (see what I did there? Clever.)

As you evolve your business and innovate, influenced by internal and external forces, so does your clientele transform over time through the same power struggles. Populations evolve through aging, relocation, diversity, social values matrix, etc. These important and sometimes swift transformations mean that your products or services focus will need to follow your clients' new status or that the offerings themselves need to transform towards new trends and interests. Your capacity to adapt steadily depends on both identifying early the new condition associated with your target customer, modify your current offering or the roadmap of your innovation offerings and finally reach and satisfy that new clientele. If you did not yet get involved in a solid strategy for clients' relations management (CRM), customer sentiment analytics and Big Data mining, get ready to dodge uppercuts.

Deus ex Machina

The time when we talk to "smart" machines for all sorts of needs has definitely arrived. Whether your partner in crime is named "Siri", "Hey Google", "Alexa" or "Cortana", you have probably experienced the human-like interaction of having a decent conversation with your digital assistant. Have we reached the level of the Turing test (Turing Test, s.d.), where we can effectively hide to a user the fact that their conversation mate is a robot? Not yet but the power of the cloud is supporting these extremely powerful algorithms, with massive research into neural networks and cognitive software, to quickly bring us where we will be very soon. And this is just the beginning because the Internet of things (IoT) is going to multiply exponentially the number of machines talking to humans and machines talking to machines.

Obviously, this creates a whole new set of challenges. Machines and humans, in the past, would require making an effort on each side to pull this

AmuseD by Innovation

off. The machine needed to use human words, syntax and, to a certain level, a form of structural analysis to understand the meaning of the sentence before trying to formulate a minimally logical answer. In the same manner, humans had to overlook the monotone, almost child-like speech patterns of the machines to keep the conversation going. There was no opportunity for emotions or complex, contextual dialog.

Most systems were based on a local on site limited computing engine. The human brain however is massively more complex. Until we had the immense computing power that is required to manage a seamless abstraction at the machine level, you were limited to the capacity you could afford. Then, the cloud came along, and it was suddenly possible to digitize the user's voice, send it to the cloud, process it with incredible efficiency and then send back the result to the user in the form of synthesized (or even digitized) speech. Today's human experience with modern bots is far superior to what was available until recently and the cloud allows this dialog to improve daily for everyone. The next frontier is now to interface human emotion, an active area of research. It will be interesting to see how it affects human-developed commerce, invented thousands of years ago. How will machines sell to humans, a very emotion-aware activity? Better yet, how will we sell to machines that have none?

If you act now, I will double your offer

Machines selling to humans need to behave more like humans, with the added benefit that they have more memory and knowledge of what they sell than most humans can. When a system like a CRM is designed to know and aggregate all the customer's interactions, including the ones that do not turn into a sale such as basic browsing, huge quantities of data can be mined to build a strong profile of the customer. This privileged knowledge is something that can be used to improve the sales process by approaching potential customers with an in-depth understanding of their interests and with a good idea of the next best action that will close the sale.

FORTUNE FAVORS THE AUDACIOUS. - ERASMUS

However, there is still a human attached to a CRM system that can support this today for one simple reason: the emotional state translated by the body language and reactions of the potential customer are very hard to read for common machines. Again, things are changing.

Machines are being thought to recognize human emotions and body language with amazing accuracy through machine learning. Soon, they may outperform us. How is this possible? Because machines can learn and detect subtle patterns based on seeing millions of different faces compared to the few thousands one meets in a human life. Just like we can train machines to associate bad penmanship with the letter "A" by having humans train it over a trial period, we can teach machines to detect interest or disdain in facial responses or voice tone.

Machines selling to machines is a different ball game altogether. How do you sell to a machine without emotions or sentiment? Surprisingly, it is deceptively simple, just not intuitive: by using what machines can process, data. This means that machines can purchase on their own using three simple rules: they are preauthorized by humans to purchase an item at a supplier, they have knowledge of suitable products and possess rules to select and purchase on their own (such as buying the lowest cost) or they can be made "confident" that the selected item is the recommended purchase through sufficient data. This last piece I find particularly interesting since this business process does not need to be predetermined or established; like humans, it can rely on reputation. Indeed, machines can use reputation data to feed their purchase analysis and go forward with the transactions – at lightning speed.

Considering that the number of machines and thus machines-to-machines conversation will soon dwarf the human variety in sheer volume, this has the potential to represent very large sales volumes very quickly. Given the availability of reputation data analysis, it can also be an extremely volatile process that companies will need to monitor tightly to manage swift massive shifts of reputation and therefore sales…

WHAT WE THINK, WE BECOME. - BUDDHA

AmuseD by Innovation

Swipe right if you like me

This new world of reputation-based referencing, which I call a meritocracy as it is based on merit (or at least what passes for it, which is debatable), is not all gloomy. Reputation and customer sentiment mining can also be useful to reduce costly expenditures associated with badly targeted product development. By providing a mechanism for customers to support an early product vision with a commitment, through models like Kickstarter and Indiegogo, it is possible to define a breakpoint where the organization can finally engage the resources and efforts required to launch a specific project with minimal risks. This model can be very disruptive since it can almost guarantee a market and product success even before any major manufacturing costs can be locked in, reducing the product development risk to a mere prototyping cost.

This is where prototyping takes a new role: as a marketing tool to help define the vision. It is disruptive because overnight, a small organization can carve a sustainable customer base and even possibly a dedicated loyal market niche by triggering the interest of the public. Using simple and limited resources such as 3D printing and cloud-based services, it can then create a name for itself if this product finds reception by ramping up production at scale. This can be a custom product designed for small run manufacturing with high margin or a potential mass market product with global strategic manufacturing partnerships contracts.

Nimble is the word and partnership is the name of the game. No more can we have a "not invented here" syndrome; the speed of competition is accelerating and the agility and ability to create synergies will define the success stories of tomorrow.

Chapter Summary

In this chapter, we have covered a lot of ground. We saw how customer's sentiment is more volatile than ever and how it can spread very quickly, for better or worse. If you are not investing in following your customer's opinions, someone else is and they will likely address your customer's

---

KEEP YOUR FEARS TO YOURSELF, BUT SHARE YOUR COURAGE WITH OTHERS. - ROBERT LOUIS STEVENSON

changing needs faster and better. We have also discussed the fact that machine selling, and machine purchasing are entering the fray, with modern algorithms that provide ever better customer targeted sales. With the potential for machines to have exponentially more dialogs than there are humans on the planet, this is a very important question to address. Finally, social media is here to remind us that reputation can make or break you, so you need to devote a bit of love to that special one.

AmuseD by Innovation

Chapter 13 – An obstacle course covered with landmines

Topics covered

Here we are at the end of part 3. Now that you have an idea, that you have figured how you can make it happen, that you know who you will pitch it to and when you want to make it happen, everything should be just great right? Well, almost. It turns out that you may have to deal with one more little thing called Murphy's Law. Look it up, it's a doozy. If, by chance, you have never heard of it, then I suggest that you stop reading this book and head directly to the casino. You most likely have the luck of the Irish and all you need is a set of dice and a few bucks to achieve success.

A bit of history

Going back to Murphy's Law and all its siblings (here's a new one for you: Bourgoin's Law states that "before you have finished exploring all of Murphy's Laws derivatives, there will be a new one showing up on the Internet."), you need to accept faith for what it is: even the best laid plans will hit bumps because "it there is a chance it can go wrong, it surely will". I suspect this is probably why nobody ever managed to organize a focus group on pessimism.

Let me tell you a story about another trip I organized with my family.

First, I need to explain that this French-Canadian boy married into a very nice traditional Italian family. As such, we do not travel light – ever. Usually, I try to keep our food stockpile to a week's ration per one-day trip. I sincerely believe that even if we cross the desert and the car breaks down on the side of the road, we will get help before we need to rely on cannibalism. And so, one day, I decided to bring my wife, kids and my in-laws on a one-week trip to a rented home facing the ocean. The road was well known to me, and I could manage it in my trusted minivan.

So, we drove for about five hours, without killing each other. The six of us would have had plenty of space were it not for the fact that I had lost my fight that day and we were carrying probably two weeks' worth of food...

I BELIEVE THAT IF ONE ALWAYS LOOKED AT THE SKIES, ONE WOULD END UP WITH WINGS. - GUSTAVE FLAUBERT

AmuseD by Innovation

This instant marks the appearance of Murphy's Law. As I was driving, I noticed that the other side of this two-way scenic road was obstructed by the wing of a "ginormous" windmill being delivered to a local windfarm; I chose to keep my distance from this behemoth. This was unfortunately also the moment when the car in front of me noticed a gift shop and decided to put the brakes and turn right after this contraption's crossing. The two following seconds felt like hours.

I calculated that while I might have enough breaking distance to avoid the car in the front, the one following me from behind would decide our fate. The road on the left was a no-go and so I chose the next option: I pumped my breaks to signal the car in the back to slow down, then reduced my speed enough to hit the unpaved roadside on the right, rocked my wheels left and right to create maximum friction but not enough to roll and ended my journey only a few feet passed my forward neighbour. Since I was next to a ditch and my car axle was wrecked, the car slowly dropped in the hole, sending many things flying through the windows. I was the only one hurt with a scar on my forehead, from the drop in the trench.

The car was finished. First day of vacation. With help, I ended up renting another minivan to finish our so desperately needed holiday before taking care of the insurance. We picked up our journey where we left off with this new vehicle on our way to our salute the following day. I thought it could only get better from here. Moments like these are when you gain wisdom, folks. Stopping at a gas station to fill up, I was checking this unfamiliar vehicle to see if everything was in order. My wife, used to opening the side door of our old minivan electrically, did not think twice to push this one open manually in one full swing.

The next thing I remember was my better half, asking me what I was doing lying on the floor of the gas station looking like I was taking a nap. It took a good minute before I could sit up and realize that, in this position, the side door of this minivan corresponded oddly with the location of the horrible oozing I felt on my forehead, under my baseball cap.

MOTIVATION WILL ALMOST ALWAYS BEAT MERE TALENT. - NORMAN RALPH AUGUSTINE

AmuseD by Innovation

To this day, I support the fight against multiple concussions in sports.

Truth is, you can plan as much as you want, problems will happen. Your flexibility will dictate how you recover to continue your journey. The moral of my story is that if you plan to launch an innovation initiative in your business, plan to slay the dragon. Be optimistic about the results but make sure to have the right armor to survive the ordeal. And then add some more, for good measure. Remember, failing an innovation project fast is acceptable if you have adopted an innovation culture but failing at adopting innovation can eventually be fatal. If this is your first innovation project, it needs to create confidence and thus requires more attention to avoid failure.

Playing catch with nail guns

Chapter 6 talked a lot about the human capacity to cope with change. Humans are an interesting species. We are the best at adapting to many environments and events, having survived, over the centuries, countless disasters and inhospitable locations. Yet we struggle with change. This, I believe, has to do with our capacity to appreciate stability as well; we love to stay in our comfort zone.

Except status quo in business means to sit down while the race keeps on going. A culture of change is not an easy thing to introduce because change is synonym with effort, the alchemist's "Magnum Opus" (Magnum Opus, s.d.). Humans' ability to deal with the rate of change is possibly limited by our most common weakness, laziness, the source of greatest resistance. Fortunately, there is hope. While managing change is definitely a good strategy in any major undertaking, realize that as the old joke states: "it takes only one psychiatrist to change a lightbulb; however, the lightbulb needs to want to change."

So, the secret to embracing change is to desire it. Preferably, it should be some gain that is also at the individual level, not just the organization. This book is called "AmuseD by Innovation" for a reason: it needs to be an enjoyable and even fun experience to gain access to new cool technologies. Let employees use the 3D printers for their own personal use! Let them

DESERVE YOUR DREAM. - OCTAVIO PAZ

borrow and fly drones with their family for the weekends. Let them build things using your resources that they can really use and maybe, just maybe, you will find scenarios that you can develop within your business plan.

Human resistance to change is probably the most effective method to extinguish the innovation flame. I have heard many arguments on how to motivate people with the next big thing. One that comes out often is the statement "what's in it for me?" I am not a big fan of this approach. Instead, I strongly suggest twisting this around so that you offer "what can I do that will help you?" The reason is simple: people have an easier capacity to describe what is wrong in their life than what they wish to have. People will usually gain more motivation from knowing they will get rid of a problem rather than acquire something that they never really wished for.

So, my last word to you is this: avoid starting an innovation agenda until you have created interest for the individuals in your organization to embrace it.

A budget leak is not the same as cash flow

Cost is a matter of fear in every industry. Understandably, margins are thinning, competition is fierce and everything seems to be more complicated as an organization matures. Innovation, due to its undefined nature, seems to have the worst reputation because we hear about so many failures. Again, let's keep in mind that you also learn from failure. Just like when you put your first foot in a puddle of water on the street and walk home with a squeaky shoe, you learn that you should not step in a wet spot on the street unless you know how deep it is. That's useful.

Let's put this in perspective. Every year, the car industry fights a bloody battle. They introduce new features in their car with each new model, without reinventing the entire car. This probably represents only between one and two percent of changes every year, which may end up being perceived as over fifteen to twenty percent of changes for a typical family that replaces a car every few years. While this evolution is significant and is not without costs, the designers and engineers behind these transformations account for a fraction of the cost of manufacturing these cars in volume. Yet, for this proportionally small investment, their contribution is immense because without these new exciting improvements, they might lose your business on the next purchase.

To put it in another way, innovation's cost is nowhere near the cost of not innovating and eventually losing business to competitors.

I sense a disturbance in the force

Political and/or economic instability is an external force that is unpredictable and devastating. As I write these lines, the United States is in election season with some of the most opposing views ever endorsed in its history; the results may have lasting repercussions. Situations like these need to be managed when you pilot a global organization that spans multiple economies and political landscapes.

Nobody can predict the future. In fact, most futurologists will tell you that there is one more thing that is as sure as death and taxes: they will be wrong at some point. Predicting the future is a Schrödinger's cat: until you lift the box, the cat is in an unknown state which can be summed up as both dead and alive. The future is analogous to the quantum state and studying it actually can decide its final state!

Logic states that you will survive a disaster if you have an escape plan. Preferably, a ladder should be closest to you to reach it easily. The same goes for innovation ideas that rely on crossing political borders or economic influence; if most of it was planned with worst case scenarios and alternatives, you should work it out fairly easily. If political instability looms on the horizon, I would strongly suggest looking for local alternatives which can be easier to reach and transact with, should things go wrong. Even the technology landscape sudden changes can have repercussions that call for planned alternatives. If you decide to leverage loosely connected micro-services in the cloud to build unique products or services or use highly distributed technologies such as blockchain, know that a shockwave within these services that you depend on will impact you directly. This is where you

---

STRIVE NOT TO BE A SUCCESS, BUT RATHER TO BE OF VALUE. - ALBERT EINSTEIN

need to clearly define what partner synergy means and how it differs from partner dependency.

Crash test dummies in a car full of airbags

Since we are venturing in the political spheres of influence, it is a good time to talk about the legal aspects of innovation. While we are seeing a strong trend towards partnership, community-led information sharing and open-source, a dangerous trend is also escalating: the litigation over intellectual property. Sharing in the business world is different; it needs to consider what belongs to whom and how it can be used. Most sharing of intellectual property should be attached with legal protection in the form of a license that defines these use cases and limits of liability.

While this may seem obvious, problems do not develop when you purchase products or services that require this fine print, but when you are not aware that you are using such products or services in your innovation and end up with the litigation that comes with it. Partnership traceability is not the same as accountability, both require however a discipline of rigorous ownership management. Unfortunately, many innovation projects are killed in the womb because accountability has legal ramifications and nobody wants to open this Pandora's Box. Imagine for an instant that your innovation introduces risk that depends on another partner's product warranty. Who owns the risk?

Risk and gain go hand in hand. If your innovation benefits your partners, risk can be shared if there is a gain for them as well. If you reduce your manufacturing costs, they should save money which is an incentive to participate in this journey. If you add features, it should also improve their products as well. Look at it as if you were creating a joint venture and share your plan with your partners. They may even provide you with their feedback ahead of time since they are your customers as well.

As a general rule of thumb, every part of your project's innovations should have a clearly identified source that can be validated for its suitability with the business goals of the organization.

IF YOU CAN DREAM IT, YOU CAN DO IT. - WALT DISNEY

AmuseD by Innovation

Also worth mentioning in that regulated industries need to clearly understand the scope these regulations are meant to accomplish and how they should be applied. In today's business world, we are quick to apply industry regulations to protect our business health. Yet we fail miserably to question what these regulations are meant for and if they should even be challenged. Regulations are built to provide a framework of measurable and verifiable activities that guarantees a specific outcome within a set of acceptable limits. There will be a time when those regulations start making less sense as your industry evolves. It will be your responsibility to push those boundaries and be at the forefront of evolution at the risk of letting others define the limits of these capabilities. If you can only do good, be bold!

License to thrill

I would like to end this chapter by explaining why it is essential to make a clear distinction between a strategic plan and a tactical plan. I believe both are necessary and should be in every major project, as part of your innovation initiative. This discussion is about the cohesion of all your organization capabilities into one formidable force. Everybody has a contribution to your innovation agenda; it is to your advantage to let everyone participate and contribute in their own ways. You should give them a license to thrill you with their perspective of your innovation vision.

The strategic overall goal

The strategic plan stands to define the general HOW point of view of WHAT you want to achieve in terms of goals and apply these actions to WHO it makes sense. This is defined as a statement of the overall goal that you are launching and paints a broad canvas that avoids any details. It should align with both your mantra and your mission. For example, this could be stated as "we want to reduce our human risk and employees' injuries by introducing automation into our business with the additional benefit that we will be able to grow our yield and increase our market share globally."

AmuseD by Innovation

The tactical objective

The tactical plan will have a more granular approach to defining the innovation initiative. Often, it may have different variations of tactical actions that vary for different locales, regions or even departments. This is to account for different realities that may affect the way we achieve the strategic goal, which remains the same for the entire organization. This can go so far as to affect the WHERE and the WHEN of the strategy's details for a specific scenario, acceptable as long as the strategic vision remains.

To apply this to our previous example, we might want to execute the strategic plan by introducing automation with manufacturing robots in a rich country like the United States to increase the productivity and reduce expensive injuries, thus yielding a cost-effective model to this region of the globe. However, in a plant located in a poor country where labor is less costly and regulations are not as well defined, automation of processes required to guarantee employee well-being by enabling best practices through machine-controlled safety measures may hold the same benefits where it can protect the workers and increase their ability for excellence.

Obstacles can slow you down but never stop you

Finally, I would like to end this chapter on a positive note. "The pessimist sees the difficulty in every opportunity. The optimist sees the opportunity in every difficulty." Remember that you are the only one who can be the agent of change in your life. You are given every day an opportunity to make others benefit from the innovation you possess and it's your choice to be selfish and keep this great knowledge for yourself or make others benefit from that insight. Everybody has something to contribute and when we work together, we can move mountains.

Chapter Summary

This chapter was one of the most challenging of the book and one of the most important to ensure your innovation success. Trying to summarize it is almost futile so I will keep it to the basics. For your innovation to succeed, you need to include into your plan all the specifics regarding the

AmuseD by Innovation

management of people's expectations, to structure a reasonable budget, plan for external forces outside of your control by keeping a tight leach and a lifeboat nearby, attach the proper legal and regulatory requirements and finally actively involve your people. Successful innovation is a team sport.

Part 4 – Something new, something blue...

"For sure, Sir Gutenberg, you ARE the genius who made it possible to print hundreds of Bibles to get rich. I am just wondering if it might be easier to just print money..."

Summary

We are coming to the end of our journey. You probably now have a decent idea about how you could innovate in your business, but a few details might still be sketchy. This section of the book will try to give you tools to safeguard and nurture the spark that has been developing. We will explore how we can plan with maximum effectiveness this innovation agenda. We will review the most common obstacles to reach your innovation goals and how to avoid them. Finally, we will look at ways of improving your innovation idea, to make people stop and pay attention.

AmuseD by Innovation

Chapter 14 – Interdimensional travels

Topics covered

In this chapter, we will emphasize a good business practice: cover our proverbial buttocks! Innovation is mighty cool, but it is an extreme sport. This can be traced to a common misconception: "accept failure if you fail fast". I prefer to accept failure as a minor step-back to success. To do this, you need a level of awareness and autonomy that rivals the best frontiersmen. Hazards can take you down – unless you have a plan. I will suggest ways to keep you on the road, with your (favorite) limbs intact.

A bit of history

My brother has a cool job: he is a professional illusionist. His daily work involves thinking about methods to amaze people with contraptions that are utterly impossible. He has been doing this for the last forty years and I am still astonished at how much he can surprise me even after having been exposed to a lot of his fabricated miracles my entire life.

But the secret about shocking people is that good illusionists can always count on one thing from their public: we are only human. We have five senses and one brain, and they can be quickly choked by information overload, putting us in a very susceptible mode to be mesmerized. This is not a secret, it's a fact! No magicians will get angry at me for revealing this since you cannot help it; you will still get caught despite knowing it.

Which brings me to my next subject. I will explore why innovation requires multiple points of view, thinking and extrapolating on many levels. We will analyze why many project leaders become distracted by data overload and how planning and timing require special care to avoid these pitfalls.

Multidimensional thinking

This may sound like some kind of cheesy science-fiction plot but innovation planning, from the ignition point of inspiration to the actual implementation, requires following paths in multiple dimensions. I am obviously not talking about traveling in a fictitious spaceship but rather about the ability to map

---

THE BEST PREPARATION FOR TOMORROW IS DOING YOUR BEST TODAY. - H. JACKSON BROWN, JR.

many pathways and milestones so that we can execute a project successfully. Depending on the scale of the innovation you chose to implement, this timeline of events can literally morph while you are actively working at it. This is because you are working at assembling components for a future product or service that can have parts that are available today, parts that may be available soon, parts that are not yet available or even parts that are only probable at this point. This presents unique challenges that require special talents.

We explained earlier the risks attached to economic or geopolitical changes that might affect your project plan. In fact, there are many other situations that can have adverse effects, and a project manager will usually define a critical path to track the most important risks associated to this project. But how do you define the impact on the project of a component availability that does not yet exist? Do you assume that it will be available and plan accordingly (the optimistic approach) or assume for your project the possibility that it may never be accessible (the pessimistic approach)?

Going back to our physics analogy, I suggest that you take the quantum approach: it is and it is not at the same time. What this means is that you should create a virtual milestone that is movable in time, for which dependencies should be loosely coupled. Ideally, this volatile milestone of uncertainty should provide "improvements" to the original idea but not be dependent on it. You should have alternate paths around this decision point that define actual impacts on the outcome (in the form of innovation importance, business goals and/or economic impacts). This also means that this virtual milestone may be moved in time and could find its way in a different place in the project itself; one might even choose to push back the inclusion of this milestone in a future improvement for a next generation of this product or service.

It is essential to keep in mind that innovation has a cost. You may hear often that it is acceptable to fail if you fail fast, but what this means is that you need to fail at the concept level, not in production. When products or

AmuseD by Innovation

services are scaled for massive manufacturing or delivery, changes can be very costly and let's not talk about recalls. Scrutinised quality testing is essential, which can also put you at risk if time is of the essence in a competing scenario. Remember, innovation that works is progress and innovation that fails is fatal. I strongly recommend pushing back on the riskier options because customer trust is hard to recover once lost, even if your innovations are industry changing. History is filled with great innovations that ultimately benefited competitors (if you have never watched "Tucker: The Man and His Dream", I strongly recommend it) so my message to you is to ensure that your innovation delights your customers.

With a clearly defined innovation project plan and with a critical path built with alternate "virtual milestones" of improvements paths, you can achieve the success you crave and more, if the stars align. Better yet, multiple dimensions planning may be the most effective approach to undercut your competitors who are eyeing similar plans but are not flexible in their design to introduce at the last minute newly available breakthroughs.

Innovation is continuous improvement on steroids

Not being able to fit every possible new idea into your innovation is not a bad thing. In fact, it may help you in the long run to determine what will be included next in the upcoming iterations of your offering. As you know, a product maturity cycle involves initial customer curiosity, discovery, interest, maximum product reach and, unfortunately, customer fatigue and finally product indifference. This is probably one of the most compelling reasons to introduce innovation into a product or service line: to reinvigorate that customer's interest and build up customer loyalty (for another cycle at least). Customer boredom is your fiercest enemy; you need to create hype and make customers stop and take notice.

Product lifecycle

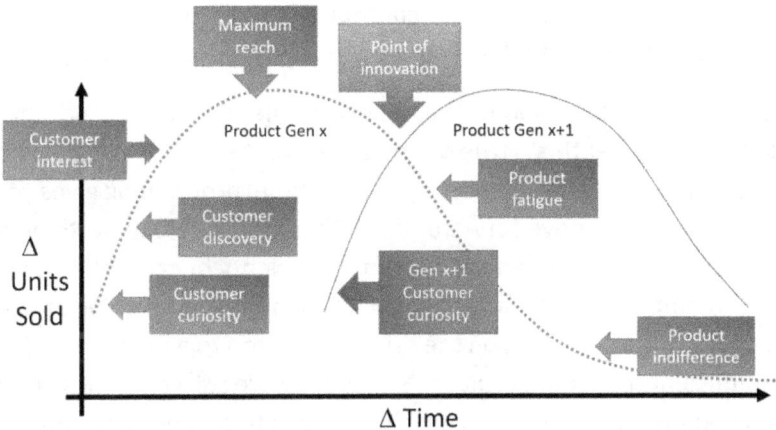

The innovations that will come out of the inspirations you trigger need to create excitement to catch that next wave of customer interest which ultimately means that you have to understand your customers' current mindset. In fact, another challenge in multiple dimensions planning is to forecast accurately the customers' interests in the near future since your innovation's implementation will happen months or maybe even years from now. As a customer's interest changes, you must detect this momentum early to track a possible timeline for your next innovation's timely introduction. You may have to anticipate this decline by analyzing possible outcomes from the current consumption model of your offering and explore what might become the next wave.

Wash, rinse, repeat

Because product maturity is a cycle, expect to be on the lookout for opportunities to introduce innovation on a regular basis. Even well-established products and service lines are likely to be disrupted in the future due mostly to synergistic and self-amplifying innovations: these are innovations that contribute to accelerate development of more innovations. Especially disrupting is the democratization of empowering technologies like the cloud, 3D printing and automation which are comparable to providing

AmuseD by Innovation

WMDs to a small belligerent nation: large scale damage in little time that can cripple the strongest. These will contribute to create an atmosphere of product enhancements that will create pressure on every industry.

Remember our story about the children, the engineers and the egg challenge? Whether this is true or not is irrelevant since the most important part is the message: given a short amount of time, prototyping gives you the fastest response to move forward, if not the most accurate. Nothing really replaces physical implementation, even after plenty of calculations; we can use supercomputers to evaluate the effects of a car impact going at 100 kph (60 mph) hitting a brick wall on the driver's skeleton to a fairly accurate level given sufficient time. But despite this capability, we still verify these theories with actual measurements of smashing a car with a dummy and looking at the results. Breaking a few eggs is the best way to make an omelet.

There are very few substitutes for prototyping when you need actionable results. Best of all, you can now simulate and prototype faster than ever. This also implies that you can explore less obvious venues: as the book says, amuse yourself, play creative scenarios. This cycle of iterations and prototypes will shape the roadmap of your product or service line. A roadmap and/or evolution is often needed because the vision is too big to be executed in one pass. Define these milestones in time and create both before and after steps that are manageable. If one step seems too hard to reach, think about what your goal is and not what you want -- this might allow you to reach acceptable levels of alternatives (90-95% of your goal for instance) using simpler or more accessible means. Prototyping and playing are keys of iterating quickly toward a better product/service.

The Fair shooting gallery

So far, we have defined a main roadmap built around a critical path supported by alternate virtual paths and milestones. Great work, but we forgot one thing: we are guilty of assuming that we know our itinerary.

Indeed, what if your innovation inspiration is just that: an idea with no actual defined plan to make it real? Strangely enough, such an idea can become a

EITHER I WILL FIND A WAY, OR I WILL MAKE ONE. - PHILIP SIDNEY

AmuseD by Innovation

most compelling innovation. Many stories exist from Silicon Valley's startups regarding industry leaders who announced vaporware products that were not yet possible, with the firm belief that they would make them real very soon. While this seeding is risky and can backfire if sponsors expect a firm timeline, it can also play to motivate your organization in meeting these aggressive deadlines by embracing this vision. Science-fiction as a knack for capturing the imagination and becoming science-fact if the idea is very attractive.

If you are seduced by this strategic move that can disrupt industries and markets, I recommend these simple principles: know your risks in advance, avoid providing committed timelines and define a vision target that is flexible to allow it to be revisited on a regular basis, as time goes on. Mars may not see humans in the foreseeable future but if we do not define it as an actual target, we will never push ourselves to colonize other planets. The dream is the goal, and it becomes clearer as you get nearer.

True innovation is a chimera

Besides, innovating is about changing the expected behavior of a product or service to improve it. It is not exceptional to see an innovation idea actually composed of several smaller innovations.

For instance, one could develop a new vehicle frame that is 3-D printed to provide a few customizations; this defines the main innovation solution. The concept can introduce other secondary ideas that will benefit this on-demand capacity: the printing process can include mesh technology in this common basic skeleton, facilitated by 3-D printing, to create new lightweight physical shapes that are original AND stronger than the traditional ones, spreading the forces over many tension points. One could push this further by implementing responsible innovation patterns using better eco-friendly material (bamboo fiber 3-D resin?) The point is that advancements in technology can benefit in more than one way; your innovation inspiration should be allowed to mature, in one single instance or as part of a roadmap of evolution.

ONE WAY TO KEEP MOMENTUM GOING IS TO HAVE CONSTANTLY GREATER GOALS. - MICHAEL KORDA

AmuseD by Innovation

Anticipation instead of provocation

Let's imagine a scenario. Taking a walk on the street, an individual decides to provoke you into a fight. Unless this person touches you, there is no genuine assault. If you choose to make the first move, you are the one at fault. The best you can hope for is to anticipate the next moment and choose the appropriate reaction, whether it is to retaliate or leave the scene. The difference is significant: timing is essential. Provocation is an action that is carried out before the time is right. Anticipation is the art of extrapolating many future scenarios and selecting the one that seems the most appropriate in the timeline expected.

Third time's the charm

I will conclude this chapter by taking a moment to talk about the speed of innovation. As mentioned earlier a few times in the book, people can and are often the weakest point in innovation speed; it challenges people and contributes to push them forward faster than expected or tolerable. This can affect the people in your organization or your customers. Sometimes, people are just not ready for the kind of innovation that you introduce.

Take for instance the story of the microwave oven. Despite its very early discovery not long after the Second World War, it was only marketed to households in the early 70's. Within fifteen years, the spread of microwave ovens grew in US homes to reach 25% by 1986. However, many households were still reluctant to own one, out of the fear of radiation to people or from irradiated foods. The market took another ten years to reach 90% through carefully crafted messages directed at potential buyers to rebuff this misconception. Fear of radiation was a major factor in slowing the adoption of this very useful household product.

Clearly, the advantage of being first on the market with an innovative product or service contributes immensely to the reputation of market leadership from the business that introduced it. It is however important to gauge if maximum penetration of the market is necessary as products that

---

PERSEVERANCE IS NOT A LONG RACE; IT IS MANY SHORT RACES ONE AFTER THE OTHER. - WALTER ELLIOT

predate the capacity of customers to adopt them can be perceived as low performers and may be retired before they can reach their full potential.

Chapter Summary

Innovation is a never-ending cycle of improvements with clearly defined evolution steps. This path is like a tree with branches that all lead to the same destination. To avoid climbing a branch that is a dead end, you need to develop the skills to identify weaker links and either choose to avoid them or plan to jump to another nearby branch to continue your climb. This requires an ability to recognize early warnings: branches that are still too weak to climb or too timeworn and brittle. To keep options opened is to climb many branches at the same time, sharing many innovations in one product; if one branch is compromised, simply continue your ascension on the remaining ones, with a lookout for new forks to explore.

AmuseD by Innovation

Chapter 15 – Making this a social affair

Topics covered

It is said that a company can only meet one of three ends: it will thrive, it will be acquired or it will die. We already established that survival is linked to innovation, and this requires great inspiration, which you now have plenty. In this chapter, we will explore the next phase: starting the actual project. As the old saying goes, there is strength in numbers and project initiation will benefit from strategic partners' contributions. As innovations compete, your offerings become the sum of your innovations and those of your partners merged together. Thus, picking the right ally is critical to developing a strong competitive offering. Understanding the new dynamics of partnership to succeed and to manage the pressure of launching your next innovation agenda is paramount.

A bit of history

I mentioned earlier that I have an older brother who is an illusionist. Recalling the stories from our youth, I have come to realize that magicians like to push the boundaries and limits that keep most ordinary folks in line. I suspect that's why a lot of them end up as escape artists. Let me explain.

When we were kids, my parents would on occasion go out for dinner and hire a babysitter to watch over us. After a while, it became clear to my parents that this would become difficult to manage because five years separate my brother and I; it was getting harder to find babysitters that were significantly older than my brother. And so, they decided one day to allow us to stay by ourselves for the night. We lived in a quiet town and the likeliness of us being at risk was rather slim so they figured that we should be mature enough to avoid doing anything stupid. Obviously, my parents greatly underestimated our innate talent for getting into trouble.

As it turns out, after they left, we got along as well as two siblings with a very different stage of immaturity can. Like the two young cubs that we were, we pushed each other's buttons to see how far we could go, which proved to be just enough to get ourselves out of the house. It is amazing how, in the face

---

LET US MAKE OUR FUTURE NOW, AND LET US MAKE OUR DREAMS TOMORROW'S REALITY. - MALALA YOUSAFZAI

of adversity, the worst of enemies can become the best of allies. And so, my brother and I agreed for a momentary truce while we dealt with our now common foe, the dreaded locked doors of our home.

We decided to collaborate on finding how to get back in the house while the sun was setting, knowing fully well that if the darkness would not end us, Mom and Dad would surely take care of this upon their return. My brother, the ever so limits-breaking teen that he was, soon realized that we could not penetrate wood, cement nor steel. Glass was a different matter but shattering a window would not contribute to our survival when our folks would discover the damage. No, we needed a way inside that was accessible and preferably concealable. Our salvation came in the form of a window screen left open, barely larger than a can of paint, by which my younger head and my then slender body could make the transition. We immediately endeavored to open the screen and push me through. It was simple enough afterwards for me to walk back to the door, unlock it and claim our freedom! The fact that we are still both here today is a testament to my brother's skill to fix the screen and keep our parents oblivious to the subterfuge.

There are two morals to this story. First, let's agree that given the right circumstance, anyone can become allies and provide the right assets to reach a common goal, even long-time foes. Likewise, collaboration and especially partnership are skills that are essential in today's highly competitive landscape and concessions are sometimes necessary. The second moral of this story is that screens do not offer good protection; ensure that your windows are locked when you leave the house…

Partnerships and Frenemies

Partnership is a fleeting thing. Ask anyone who lived through a divorce or broke up from a long-standing relationship and they will all agree that they never expected to separate when they first started together. Nobody does (that is 0%, for if they did, that would never have counted as a relationship to begin with). In business, strategic partnerships have legal implications which make them feel a lot more like a marriage than just moving in together. You need to know what you are bringing into the relationship and what you will keep if you break apart. Given the implications, it's no wonder that a lot of people prefer to avoid marriage.

Except, there is strength in numbers. At numerous occasions, it has been proven that the best innovations were strongly supported by strategic partnerships. The name of the game is speed of execution and whatever means you use to get to the finish line faster should be considered; the "not invented here" syndrome is not an option anymore.

In fact, today's market growing strategies can often create all sorts of very odd partnership scenarios. In some cases, your new venture in a market that was traditionally the turf of a partner may create frictions if you plan on growing that influence in their space. The same goes for organizations that you used to compete with that you now need to work with to fight back a larger predator. This created the term "frenemies" (friends-enemies).

How do you choose to partner in a strategic way with organizations that could turn on you at any opportunity if you absolutely need to partner? I suggest proceeding in the same way that you would proceed to select a mate that will be your partner for life: carefully. Legal implications, the careful understanding of what is brought into the relationship and what will come out of it at its dissolution are all parts of this conversation. Most important of all, before settling in with someone, understand what is to gain from both parties; you should preferably gain the same as the other party since an uneven balance may tip the situation in one's favor, dooming the relationship before it bears fruits.

Finally, I strongly recommend looking at this collaboration as a synergistic relationship, not parasitic. What I mean by this is that this relationship should both make you stronger than functioning separately but should not create a dependence. If one of you or both cannot pursue your innovation goals without the other, unforeseen partnership changes such as partner financial state fluctuation, undisclosed alliances or even acquisitions may put your dependency under scrutiny, even possibly be fatal to your innovation

---

SUCCESS USUALLY COMES TO THOSE WHO ARE TOO BUSY TO BE LOOKING FOR IT. - HENRY DAVID THOREAU

strategy. Innovation dependency is not much better than no innovation at all.

Fear of failure is success underachieved

"Fear is the mind killer." This statement is taken from one of my favorite science-fiction books, Frank Herbert's *Dune*. In this storyline, the Bene Gesserit, sort of a warped nun's congregation, uses this litany to control their inner fear, to keep a cool head. I surprise myself sometimes repeating this as if I was an actor in this story because I use it to remind myself that fear is a survival mechanism; if my life is not in danger, I should be strong enough to overcome this fear.

I want to talk about fear because even with a very good inspiration, it is too easy to convince yourself that this is an impossible dream and then never go forward. In fact, it is possible to create mental blocks that keep you from exploring ideas that are the most interesting, keeping you out of the most challenging concepts. I started this book with a radical notion: I tested you to see if you could keep an open mind by talking about a very controversial subject, the Bigfoot legend. I could have chosen a thousand others and made sure not to ruffle your feathers, but I knew that going in this precarious topic would trigger a reaction. You need to be able to do the same to yourself every day if you want to innovate. Impossible is not static because time can make it possible; it is instead highly improbable at the moment.

Given this theorem, you have to be able to control your anxiety and convince yourself that innovating is developing something that is never finished, much like a perfectionist. You simply accept to run out of time. This is the correct way to allow your mind to wander and freely create without binding yourself to the laws of nature.

The writer's block, this incapacity to generate new ideas, might hide more than just an attitude problem. In a research on the limbic system area of the brain that houses core mental processes such as emotions, the neurologist Alice W. Flaherty (Writer's block, s.d.) suggested that under stress, the human brain may *"shift control from the cerebral cortex to the limbic*

THERE IS NOTHING I DO WELL THAT I CANNOT DO BETTER WITH HELP. - ME

AmuseD by Innovation

system." Because the limbic system manages instinctual processes, a person's creative capabilities may be suppressed by their survival instinct. This might explain why, under pressure to deliver a new novel for a deadline, a writer will not be able to function, worried by a constant reminder of the consequences of failure.

Although this research is still ongoing, it points to a link between fear of failure and the capacity to imagine. What this means is that as long as there is a fear of consequences, that creative process may be hindered. To alleviate this, I recommend to not only avoid stress by reducing failure to an acceptable level but in fact to embrace it, by developing a culture where failure is necessary to pinpoint flaws and achieve greater perfection. This process should define a low cost to that failure that is not zero but remains tolerable, so that it is registered by the brain as a factual stage that is part of the normal process. I mentioned earlier in the book how children often outperform adults with imagination; it may have to do with their limited conceptualization of constrains but it may also have a lot to do with the fact that they do not register consequences the way we do.

Procrastination is the cancer of success

Sometimes, imagination works against you. You can invent as many reasons as you need to keep yourself from walking into the unknown. Innovating is breaking the status quo. If you wait for earth-shattering events to happen, chances are, you will end up disappointed. When it comes to innovation, you are shaking the tree, you create the disruption. Because this process forces you to think outside of the box, you need to break the standard bounds of your work. If you procrastinate, you are letting other events interfere. Innovation should be your priority, and non-linear thinking should always be attached to your innovation goals.

I encourage you to stimulate yourself rather than wait for the "right" moment. If you are expected to innovate and have an interesting idea that is in need of a starting point, your best option is to immerse yourself into an innovating environment to expose you to positive reinforcement. Explore

---

LOOKING AT SMALL ADVANTAGES PREVENTS GREAT AFFAIRS FROM BEING ACCOMPLISHED. - CONFUCIUS

the tools you have. Play with new technology. Read about innovation to invigorate your interests. By exposing yourself to more innovation, you will find greater motivation to push back any attempt to deviate from your goal. You will focus on breaking down this large project into smaller manageable objectives.

Some organizations even elect to create startups, external campuses and other detached locations dedicated to outsiders and their unique requirements; my take on this is that innovation should not be an outside looking in approach but instead an inside looking out. Innovation should be embraced at all levels of the organization, to develop a culture and a community of curiosity, exploration, discovery and sharing.

Don't waste any time, use these opportunities to read, play and exchange. You cannot learn as much by yourself as you can learn as a group.

Innovation is something exciting, never seen before

The act of creation comes from inspiration, and this book is a useful tool to help you ignite this spark, where you provide the oxygen to fire the flame. For a product or service to innovate, it must break new grounds, use new technologies or materials and hopefully deliver a user experience that is fresh and unique. It all starts with an idea, followed by a maturing process that gives it life and prototypes that give it form. In the center of this, there is a will to make things better, to improve something where others are satisfied with what they have today. The Rolling Stones song should be your call to action: "*I can't get no satisfaction 'cause I try and I try and I try and I try*" ...Keeping trying as if you were never fully satisfied, you can only improve in ways you never imagined.

Recall the mantra, your reason for existing. You want to dramatically improve on your current product or service, not through incremental changes but through radical changes. You want to attract attention and lead your customer to a delightful unique experience. Your brand, which is clearly identifiable to you, must be omnipresent but the core of the change must be

AmuseD by Innovation

associated with your innovation if you wish to truly disrupt the market (Lean Innovation design, s.d.).

Chapter Summary

Accelerate to stop playing catch up and stay in pole position. This is clearly what you should retain from this chapter. You need to avoid any excuse to start your innovation agenda and create that purposeful environment that will stimulate innovation, through exploration, competition and interaction. Time is of the essence and if this means to build strategic partnerships, think about starting the proper conversations early to avoid problems later. Be warned, your first innovation success should be marked with a surgeon general warning on the package: highly addictive...

Chapter 16 – Pin the tail on the donkey

Topics covered

Hard to believe but we have reached the end of our journey, the last chapter of this book. Here, we will try to put everything we have covered together and glue this into a mosaic of knowledge that you can use to enrich your innovation intentions. I will suggest workshops and methods to improve your original inspiration and let you build on this solid foundation. The best part of this is that if the suggested workshops do not match you needs, you can now innovate to develop your own!

A bit of history

Now that we've come to the conclusion of this book, it is time for me to divulge the secret to success with innovation, which has been known since the dawn of time to achieve more in life: don't believe anyone who tells you "No". Being human is also about the fact that we want something better for ourselves and rejecting "no" for an answer is the reason we went to space and that we have explored the depths of the ocean floor. Now, I will explain how you can make the best use of the knowledge shared in this book. Think of it as your reward for staying with me this long.

And if you're part of the crowd that skips to the last chapter of a mystery novel to get a glimpse of who the murderer really is, hopefully, this will whet your appetite to start reading this book from the beginning.

Light a fire with a spark (not literally)

I keep coming back to the notion that you must have an open-mind and avoid the word "impossible". It is imperative that the vision, not the ability to deliver on the vision, leads this process. Keep the process of viability for later: many roads lead to Rome and sometimes the standard method that seems obvious can be short-circuited by new means that were not surfaced before; this is where new efficiencies (innovative as well) can combine into new wonderful ways.

IT IS BY ACTS AND NOT BY IDEAS THAT PEOPLE LIVE. - ANATOLE FRANCE

AmuseD by Innovation

Naysayers will always be around. They are actually needed because without them, we would likely be the people who jump off a building with a sheet to invent the parachute and instead leave a stain on the pavement. These people can offer healthy criticism for the wackiest ideas and give a good vital shot of reality. However, these people are not the critics of your movie, they are opinions and should be taken as such. Mature your idea before exposing it to tougher crowds, you will find the conversation more aligned towards improvement than contempt. Indeed, it is your responsibility to engage in a healthy debate to win your cause.

This debate should revolve around what needs to be done to explore this project further, in its form or another, into a fully-fledged innovation plan. The intent is NOT to prove its viability as you should make it clear that you do not have enough data to prove or disprove your theory. As was mentioned abundantly in this book, new technology appears all the time and the possibilities change daily. If, however, you do have a debate, it should be centered on agreeing on a set of goals to achieve, which logically should be the same for the entire organization. The WHY and the WHAT is the center of that conversation and the HOW needs to be pushed aside as part of the discovery and research process.

Ten times a googolplex

Google calls this methodology the 10x process, which means that the idea needs to grow 10 times bigger and better before it can be scaled down and requires a viability review. The reason is simple: it needs to break away from very simple easily accessible ideas and thus, leapfrog competition. To do this, it tries to describe the idea in six words or less in order to clarify it and reach a consensus of the goal to secure everyone's backing. Next comes the development of the idea where everyone in the team writes down their own perspective. All this brainstorming is then brought back in the pool (sharing, remember?) and then voted collaboratively on which one is the strongest (meritocracy, remember?). Notice that I did not mention about dropping ideas? This process is inclusive; all geared toward exploring how each idea can be improved instead of finding reasons why it cannot work. Think goals, objectives. The WHAT and the WHY. Draw your vision if you can. Stop thinking about what you know is possible, but what you wish could be done. Frederik Pferdt, Google's head of innovation and creativity, says "*Just beyond crazy is fabulous!* (Transform like a Googler, s.d.)"

Imagination is about having time to dream

Setting aside time to think is not an easy thing to do. Yet the speed of the modern lifestyle is precisely what prevents most people from unleashing their inner creativity. By letting someone get more engaged into a project, this individual often develops a special attachment to it, too often discouraged in today's business world. Passion is important in innovation because people do not work in the same spirit with something they are passionate about. It is important that they feel the innovation relates to some part of them or what they believe in, their personal mantra.

3M experimented with this concept with great success. By providing to employees one day a week to pursue light and engaging personal projects, they allowed their staff to explore on their own time, even letting them browse through years of intellectual property, some of it discarded as complete failures. One such famous case involved the recycling of a discarded weak bonding agent that had an unusual level of solubility leaving no additional thickness to paper. This individual's curiosity culminated in building small stacks of sticky paper which turned it into the Post-it™ success that it is today (Post-it Note History, s.d.).

Investing one day a week of employees' time may seem ludicrous. It scares the living daylights out of every controller in the corporate world; it sounds like a license for anarchy, paid for with ever so difficult to earn revenue dollars. You cannot blame them, it makes sense from their point of view: if you struggle to make single digit margins, burning 20% of the workforce time is certifiably insane and will make any CxO cringe.

Nonetheless, it is a sound investment if it is managed like an investment: carefully. Would you give twenty percent of your money to your stocks broker and hope for the best? I definitely hope not. You would probably give

WE HAVE IT IN OUR POWER TO BEGIN THE WORLD OVER AGAIN. - THOMAS PAINE instructions and follow-up on a regular basis. What you are aiming for is to nurture new original ideas, not open season for golfing. You should give the tools to your people to make the most of this personal time. Provide work areas to explore new technologies, enable virtual spaces to track the progress of their work and set aside time to learn and share with others. Again, Google is well-known to offer this work week structure, and it has shown impressive results (Nine principles of innovation, s.d.).

Sciences and the Arts

If you hear many people talk about creating innovation, they call it an art. I started this book explaining why I disagree with this opinion and will try to finish it by upholding why non-artists can become innovators. If you are not a born innovator, you need a methodology to trigger ideas that come to others naturally. This book's methodology will not teach you to be the equivalent of a Picasso or Van Gogh in the art of innovating, but it teaches fundamental skills that improve your natural gifts. I want you to draw better than just stick people (just assuming) by giving you the innovation equivalents of perspective, anatomy and so on. Once you have mastered these basic skills, you can then go on to developing your very own "style". Every art, whether it is music or painting or sculpting needs a base that you play with; this inspiration book was developed with this specific goal.

As a matter of fact, if you are a "gifted" individual who seems to possess limitless amounts of imagination, you can only gain from using this methodology to improve your skills. And it will eventually be useful because I have a surprise for you: that well has a bottom. It happens to every writer that at some point, ideas don't seem to pop anymore. When it happens, you need tools to re-ignite the flame by stimulating the idea generation process. That's where this book comes in handy. For this reason, I will take this moment to talk about the artist way and the scientific way of creating innovation.

AmuseD by Innovation

The artist innovation framework

The innovation artist has an indefinite goal, exploring and "catching waves" through the artist journey (very much like Apple Computer in the Jobs heydays) – they achieve many failures, but the pearls are game changers because they rarely depend on traditional established formulas and ideas. The art is fundamentally a departure from the conventional. These innovations are often "transnovations" because they specifically try to avoid the old ways.

The artist's canvas is often managed by instinct, which is another name for the basic rules that govern decisions influenced by memories, conscious or not. In many cases, the artist is very much aware of the artistic world where he or she evolves; this may shape the vision of the composition or can be used to guarantee a withdrawal from what has been done by others. Since the work is very much driven by emotions, it usually carries a specific purpose and sometimes unique esthetics. While artists brand their products to a definite style, it is not by will but mostly by habit since artists looks to explore new opportunities with every execution.

Like a great novel, the artist is motivated by generating a public's reaction, the singular user experience full of passions brought forth by the vision that is the ambition behind the product. The products that reach the same rhythms as the audience become sensations; the ones that do not resonate the same way with the targeted audience simply fail.

I call this the artist framework because the artist's process can actually be very consistent but highly unequal. There is little repeatability in the motion because the artist usually does not like predictable behavior, this is analogous to painting the same scene twice. The strength of the artist comes from the passion of the work, the clarity of the vision. If the idea can speak to the people, it holds a tremendous amount of potential energy.

If you are one of these people who can't wait to try something new, then you've got the makings of an innovator!

IN ORDER TO SUCCEED, WE MUST FIRST BELIEVE THAT WE CAN. - NIKOS KAZANTZAKIS

AmuseD by Innovation

The scientific procedural innovation framework

I believe there are only three models for innovation inspiration all based on the same general roadmap: this is what I call the OMG principle. It forms the basis of my scientific process to develop a systemic method of innovation development.

Just like in science, the scientific approach to innovation is simply a way of clearly defining steps to achieve the desired output. In this case, the steps that are defined in the "standardised" innovation journey are simply the point of origin (where you are), the destination which is your goal to achieve (what you want to do) and the path that you need to follow to morph into the destination (the journey). Because this is such a deceptively simple method and because I like to name things, I call this the OMG method (OMG, I never guessed it was that simple!).

The OMG method

The **OMG** principle is just another acronym (JAA!):

- **O: stands for the (O)rigin point** of a product or service that you own and wish to evolve/re-invent; you apply new technologies to its evolution organically through modelling and exploration.
- **M: stands for the (M)odification or (M)anipulation** of your product/service from the starting point towards a yet undefined target for a modern service/product; you explore what new technologies can contribute to transform/shape/morph this from one to the other.
- **G: stands for the (G)oal** of the new product of service as a new iteration with few previous similarities; it defines the needs and general aspects of what role it pursues; new technologies guide this vision into a solution that will structure and define the objective/goal of the result.

I THINK AN ARTIST HAS ALWAYS TO BE OUT OF STEP WITH HIS TIME. - ORSON WELLES

AmuseD by Innovation

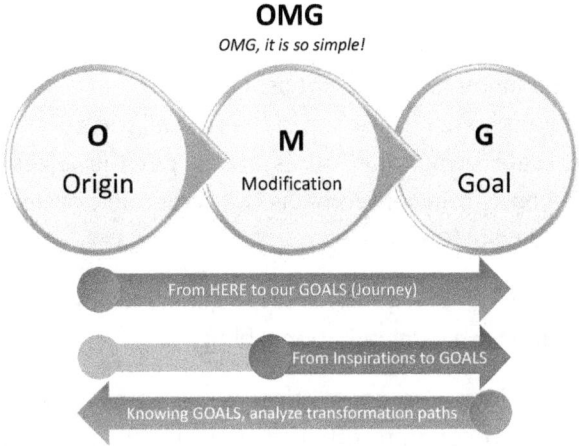

Playing with the baseball cards in chapter 11

The baseball cards (or hockey cards if you are a Canadian like me), are specifically built with a format that presents a WHY/WHAT/HOW structure to help you gather your thoughts. Most organizations and leaders can articulate fairly well their goals (the WHY) but identifying ways to realize them through new technologies and trends can be daunting, considering that so much happens everywhere all the time. This explains the WHAT and HOW sections that are purposely generic to encourage further up-to-date research once the idea has been seeded. For instance, you may have identified that using modern materials in a product line could offer benefits, but this card invites you to explore the current new meta-materials that are being offered at this very moment.

The format of the baseball card was created specifically to support many different types of workshops. They are designed to help you flow your thought process starting from a WHY set of goals or from a WHAT set of destination results with a HOW plan and suggested tools to implement this journey. The following section shows you a sample of brainstorming sessions that use these cards to spawn innovation ideas.

AmuseD by Innovation

Innovation inspiration workshop ideas

There are literally countless ways that you can use the cards to conduct your inspiration and innovation workshops. I am sure that as you go on, you will find some of your own. I have used in the past all sorts of thought-provoking ideas to generate stimulation necessary to get the juices of imagination going but the basic principle remains the same: do not discard any idea at first glance and have fun.

Here are a few of my favorite exercises to generate new ideas or enhance an initial inspiration with some additional bling.

1. **Jump points**: Use game triggers the same way authors use plot devices; to generate other ideas (this falls into the (M)odification and/or (G)oal categories):
    - Sci-Fi conceptualization: make up strange inventions or environments like the *Star Trek©* TV show that pioneered a teleportation machine as a plot device to "simplify" and "open-up" new avenues of stories. This provides a framework inspired by the cards to free up ideas and to explore "strange new ways" that can challenge and revolutionize industries. Two great examples of these are the "tricorder" medical scanning device and the "holodeck", both having served as the basis for real contemporary research.
    - Ideas breeding: create a list of strengths and capabilities in your organization and mix it with a pool of new trends in technologies taken from the baseball cards; try to "breed" them together and explore the benefits of such new aptitudes.
    - Use the "Bold Bucket": create a bucket where people will write any wild ideas they have, crimple the papers and throw them in like so much rejected thought. Then, open the anonymous contributions within a group (think tank) and revisit them as if they were actually possible by trying to take advantage of the baseball cards ideas – don't think them through, be bold!

2. **Corporate X-Prize:** create your own X-prize contests (this falls into the (G)oal category):
   - Science Fair: Offer a prize and a chance to present ideas, inspired by the baseball cards triggers or not. Have these ideas evaluated by a panel of judges that can be internal or external to the organization to create interest and possibly invest further if the ideas are truly worth investigating.
   - Moon Race: Create a friendly competition within the organization to challenge teams of employees to come up with the best ideas to address a set of predetermined themes or corporate/market key issues.
   - Scrapbook: Pick up a set of recent newspapers' headlines and/or news websites references and clippings; start looking for articles relating to problems or events where your organization could make a difference. Explore how this could be accomplished by looking at what is available today or coming soon within your organization or by using the cards.
   - The Showcase: Because goals are very much evidence-driven (with proven statistics or through experience), launch your own concept of the TV show *"Shark Tank"* ©/ *"Dragon's Den"* ©. As a recommendation, I suggest that the judges participate to improve ideas instead of rejecting them -- who wants to swim in a shark tank, let alone go back after a bad experience?
3. **Workshops and brainstorming sessions:** conduct workshops with diversified teams that explore new technology on a regular basis, by introducing a carousel of employees in the conversations:
   - Future Perfect (this falls into the (M)odification and/or (G)oal categories): you play a reporter in the future relating this fictional success story, asking the interviewee to start answering this way: "Yes, today in <date in the future>, we <your organization> have achieved tremendous success with this new technology based on (choose a baseball card technology family

---

SUCCESS COMES WHEN PEOPLE ACT TOGETHER; FAILURE TENDS TO HAPPEN ALONE. - DEEPAK CHOPRA

picked randomly in a hat or selected in the book) by introducing <name of your fictional innovation>".
- Darwin Treehouse (this falls into the (O)rigin category): take a product and develop it into an evolution tree with branches made from either disrupting events or interesting new technology taken from the baseball cards or other sources; explore how these evolution branches fan out.
- Magellan (this falls into the (M)odification category): Start at Point A with a product or service that exists today and create a fictional point B where that service/product has been transformed 10 years later into something completely different, due to either external pressure, known tendencies or new interests. Then try to link the two points into a roadmap from point A to point B across a number of milestones using technology advances that are here today or inspired by the baseball cards.
- Utopia (this falls into the (G)oal category): List all the obstacles that block innovation or change in your business today and try to create scenarios where none of these would exist in the near future to see where they lead; evolve the business through iterations to explore this new endpoint world.
- Alternate Ending (this falls into the (G)oal category): Think out-of-the-box -- literally, conduct workshops with your current and potential customers, not just internally but also by introducing target audiences to gather feedback (even movies are sometimes influenced to create a "preferred" ending based on customer feedback during limited screening).
- Periscope (this falls into the (O)rigin category): start with data insights from modern data mining of current customer data; use powerful new data analytics or machine learning tools to identify details and patterns about your customers that you did not know you had. Investigate this insight to see if it could serve as the basis to initiate R&D of new products and services.

Remember that there are no bad techniques to generate and develop inspired innovation projects as long as you institutionalize collaboration and innovation as organizational values. When you purge bad ideas on a regular basis (through exploration), what remains improves every day.

Chapter Summary

This chapter was geared toward making sure that you take the right approach to support innovation ideas. As you have witnessed, innovating requires the skills of a master in the martial arts of creativity but practice it long enough and you too will become a sensei. My OMG method can prove quite useful when you want to outline the next steps in your innovation agenda.

While there is no perfection to innovation, I do use this (PER)sonal litany to focus my innovation values properly:
- Stay **(PER)sistent** in your approach.
- **(PER)meate** by sharing and collaborating.
- **(PER)colate** through imagination workshops and playing, with the courage to enhance and refine.
- **(PER)petuate** through a repeat cycle of improvements, ad infinitum.

In the words of the great American poet Emily Dickinson, I hope that you remember one simple rule from this book which I had great pleasure writing for you: *"fortune befriends the bold."*

I wish you the best of luck and hope to take advantage of your innovations soon.

References

4D Printing. (n.d.). Retrieved from Smithsonian Magazine: http://www.smithsonianmag.com/innovation/Objects-That-Change-Shape-On-Their-Own-180951449/

BrainyQuote - Thomas Edison. (n.d.). Retrieved from BrainyQuote: http://www.brainyquote.com/quotes/quotes/t/thomasaed109928.html

Business Mortality. (n.d.). Retrieved from Fortune: http://fortune.com/tag/business-mortality/

Chinese Martial Arts External and Internal classifications. (n.d.). Retrieved from Wikipedia.org: https://en.wikipedia.org/wiki/Styles_of_Chinese_martial_arts#External_and_Internal_classifications

CNC. (n.d.). Retrieved from Wikipedia.org: https://en.wikipedia.org/wiki/Numerical_control

Dada. (n.d.). Retrieved from Wikipedia.org: https://en.wikipedia.org/wiki/Dada

en.wikipedia.org. (n.d.). Retrieved from Wikipedia: https://en.wikipedia.org/wiki/Almas

en.wikipedia.org. (n.d.). Retrieved from Wikipedia: https://en.wikipedia.org/wiki/Industrial_Revolution#Second_Industrial_Revolution

Fortune 500 2015. (n.d.). Retrieved from Geolounge: https://www.geolounge.com/fortune-1000-companies-list-for-2015/

Kanter, R. M. (2015). *MOVE: Putting America's infrastructure back in the lead.* W. W. Norton & Company.

Lean Innovation design. (n.d.). Retrieved from Forbes.com: http://www.forbes.com/sites/sap/2016/04/07/lean-innovation-design-thinking-meets-lean-startup-for-the-enterprise/

Magnum Opus. (n.d.). Retrieved from Wikipedia.org: https://en.wikipedia.org/wiki/Magnum_opus_(alchemy)

mentalfloss.com. (n.d.). Retrieved from Mentalfloss: http://mentalfloss.com/article/63902/15-unexplored-corners-earth

Metacognition. (n.d.). Retrieved from Meriam-Webster.com: http://www.merriam-webster.com/dictionary/metacognition

MS2. (n.d.). Retrieved from Wikipedia.org: https://en.wikipedia.org/wiki/Bacteriophage_MS2

Nine principles of innovation. (n.d.). Retrieved from Fastcompany.com: https://www.fastcompany.com/3021956/how-to-be-a-success-at-everything/googles-nine-principles-of-innovation

Nirvana. (n.d.). Retrieved from Wikipedia.org: https://en.wikipedia.org/wiki/Nirvana

Plato. (n.d.). *Plato's Apology of Socrates.* Retrieved from SJSU.edu: http://www.sjsu.edu/people/james.lindahl/courses/Phil70A/s3/apology.pdf

Post-it Note History. (n.d.). Retrieved from CNN.com: http://www.cnn.com/2013/04/04/tech/post-it-note-history/index.html

QuickTake. (n.d.). Retrieved from Wikipedia.org: https://en.wikipedia.org/wiki/Apple_QuickTake

San Francisco 1906 Earthquake. (n.d.). Retrieved from Wikipedia.org: https://en.wikipedia.org/wiki/1906_San_Francisco_earthquake

Singularity. (n.d.). Retrieved from Wikipedia.org: https://en.wikipedia.org/wiki/Technological_singularity

Stocks without dividends. (n.d.). Retrieved from Fool.com: http://www.fool.com/investing/general/2013/11/10/why-dont-these-winning-stocks-pay-dividends.aspx

TEDx Berkeley Guy Kawasaki. (n.d.). Retrieved from Youtube.com: https://www.youtube.com/watch?v=Mtjatz9r-Vc

Transform like a Googler. (n.d.). Retrieved from Fastcompany.com: https://www.fastcompany.com/3061059/your-most-productive-self/how-to-brainstorm-like-a-googler

Turing Test. (n.d.). Retrieved from University of Toronto Psychology: http://www.psych.utoronto.ca/users/reingold/courses/ai/turing.html

Wikipedia HoverBoard Entry. (n.d.). Retrieved from Wikipedia.org: https://en.wikipedia.org/wiki/Hoverboard

AmuseD by Innovation

Writer's block. (n.d.). Retrieved from Wikipedia.org: https://en.wikipedia.org/wiki/Writer%27s_block

www.absolutepanda.com. (n.d.). Retrieved from AbsolutePanda.com: http://www.absolutepanda.com/news-and-blog/89.html

www.merriam-webster.com. (n.d.). Retrieved from Merriam-Webster Online English Dictionary: http://www.merriam-webster.com/dictionary/inspiration

www.phrases.org.uk. (n.d.). Retrieved from www.phrases.org.uk: http://www.phrases.org.uk/meanings/genius-is-one-percent-perspiration-ninety-nine-percent-perspiration.html

www.wikipedia.org. (n.d.). Retrieved from Wikipedia: https://en.wikipedia.org/wiki/Mountain_gorilla

www.wikipedia.org. (n.d.). Retrieved from Wikipedia: https://en.wikipedia.org/wiki/Human_evolution

Glossary

AR: augmented reality, a virtual image superimposed on actual reality to add information or context 87

B2B: business to business computer systems, a company's system can interact directly with another partner company's system for real-time transactions 80

BBS: Bulletin Board System, a computer software that was typically accessed by a modem (analog-digital network connection) and managed like a club with membership, shared services and news 22

chimera: mythical creature that was an amalgamation of many other creatures in a single beast 127

cicadas: large harmless insects between 2 and 5 cm in size (1-2 inches) and a wingspan of 18 to 20 cm (7-8 inches), known for their male courtship calls and some species living as underground nymphs only to emerge every 13 or 17 years 27

clients relations management: CRM, a computer system that is used to track customer interactions 107

computer numeric control: a mechanism by which a computer can send operational codes to a set of motors to control a milling or carving machine to sculpt into material a specific pattern 63

CxO: also called C-suite, represents a typical chief officer role such as CEO, CFO, etc. 29

entropy: quantitative measure of disorder or energy dispersal, entropy grows with a release of energy and the adoption of a more stable lowered state of energy potential 52

freemium: pricing strategy where a product or service is offered free of charge but premium features are offered for a fee 43

Generation Z: post millennial Generation, born typically between 1990 and the first decade of the second millennium; known for their digital acumen starting at a young age 22

googolplex: represents the number 10 elevated to the power googol which is itself 10 to the power 100, a googol being presumably a number larger than the number of atoms in the universe 138

AmuseD by Innovation

hoverboard: a class of personal vehicles designed to simulate or approximate the action of hovering (floating) over ground while in motion, standing like on a skateboard 33

iDevices: general term for a category of products from Apple Computer that relate to the Internet (iMac, iPod, iPhone, iPad) 15

Internet-of-Things: IoT, a class of small smart devices that can be attached or embedded to communicate to the Internet and send or receive information/commands 80

IPsec: Internet computer communication protocol with built-in support for authentication and encryption (security) 97

IPv6: modern Internet computer communication protocol with built-in support for security and very large capacity of address space for numerous devices 97

Jovian: a massive planet of the Solar System associated with the largest which is Jupiter, includes Jupiter, Saturn, Uranus and Neptune 30

Kudzu: climbing perennial vines native to Eastern Asia from which the kuzu japanese name comes from, can be invasive as they climb trees and kills them by heavy shading 27

liDar: optical equivalent of radar technology where light beams are used to detect surroundings 87

LMS: Learning Management System, a computer system for managing training and knowledge 78

Luxor: also known as the ancient Egyptian city of Thebes, popular for its many well-preserved ancient temples and monuments 36

Magnum Opus: in alchemy, the most important work that involves the transmutation of gold using the philosopher's stone 114

metacognition: the science of studying when and how to use particular strategies for learning and problem solving 50

minimum viable product: a product with the least amount of features to confirm its alignment with expectations before adding additional features 49

NFC: Near Field Communication, low-power very short distance (sometimes requires actual touch) communication technology (see also RFID) 96

Nirvana: the ultimate state of happiness and awareness in Buddhism 59

OEM: original equipment manufacturer, a company that builds its own equipment 69

Ouroboros: ancient greek symbol of a serpent or dragon eating its own tail, often representing introspection or an infinite cycle 24

Quadcopters: a type of drone made of four motors and propellers 91
reflex camera: a camera that allows a photographer to see exactly the image that will be captured by the lense using a clever mirror and prism system 41
RFID: Radio frequency identification, low power short distance communication technology (see also NFC) 96
RNA: ribonucleic acid, a complex molecule that is associated with DNA as part of the protein assembly in complex living organisms but also acts as the genes main medium for many viruses 65
ROI: return on investments, the measure by which we can defined the gain between the initial investments and their results 55
Sasquatch: legendary large hairy primate with human-like features reported living in the western United States and Canada, also called bigfoot 12
singularity: hypothetical moment in the future where all minds (human or cybernetic) are connected into a superintelligence 67
TEDx: TED conferences are non-profit freely distributed capsules of information on technology, entertainment and design (T, E and D) 59
Turing test: a blind test by which a computer system is so advanced that it can fool a human in thinking that he/she is communicating with another human 107
USB: universal serial bus, a technology developed initially in the 1990s to create a single connector multi-purpose medium for modern data interchange 37
VAR: value added reseller, a company which resells goods with additional service 76
WMD: weapon of mass destruction 126
XML: Extensible Markup Language, a syntax of data used by computer technology to exchange data that can be mutually understood by all parties 98
Yeti: legendary human-like hairy primate believed to inhabit the Himalayas, also known as the abominable snowman 12
yogi: practitionner of yoga and meditation 54

www.ingramcontent.com/pod-product-compliance
Lightning Source LLC
Chambersburg PA
CBHW071435180526
45170CB00001B/356